BLACK TRIBUNES
Black Political Participation in B

Black Tribunes

*Black Political Participation
in Britain*

Terri A. Sewell

Lawrence & Wishart
LONDON

Lawrence & Wishart Ltd
144a Old South Lambeth Road
London SW8 1XX

First published 1993

Photoset in North Wales by
Derek Doyle & Associates, Mold, Clwyd.
Printed and bound in Great Britain by
Dotesios, Trowbridge.

Contents

To my parents
Andrew and Nancy Sewell

Preface

Power concedes nothing without a demand. It never did and never will. Men may not get all they pay for in this world but they must certainly pay for all they get.

–Fredrick Douglass
African-American Abolitionist

In the autumn of 1986, I embarked on a personal and intellectual metamorphosis. It was an experience that ultimately changed the way I viewed world politics, the critical role that race plays in the international arena, and my own blackness as it relates both to my individuality and to the collective oppression of a people.

It was on cold rainy day in 1986 – the first of many such dreary, wet days – that I matriculated at one of the world's oldest institutions of higher education, Oxford University. What I remember most is the relative absence of black faces at Oxford – not just as teachers (for that is yet another problem), but as students. I found it especially disturbing that the black students who did matriculate were largely foreigners – Africans, Asians, Caribbeans and African-Americans – most of whom were deeply committed to using their skills and talents back home. With government subsidised education in England, the dearth of black British students was particularly perplexing. While I, as a black foreign student, basked in a false sense of intellectual acceptance and academic parity, black British youth were struggling against a systematic and institutional exclusion from educational and professional opportunities.

This was a battle which, in many ways, was quite familiar to me. As a black American from Selma, Alabama, I grew up with an acute awareness of the significance of the gains made in the 1960s and counted myself substantially as a beneficiary of that movement. To witness first-hand parallel injustices in the 1980s in another country was indeed shocking.

The impetus for this book stems directly from my observations and impressions of being black in Britain. I first chronicled my thoughts as a series of entries in a journal entitled 'Walking in the Footsteps of my Sister' [that is, my other – British – self], in which I wrote about how I felt being perceived as black British – at least until I spoke. It was only when I talked that I was distinguished as an American and it seemed that then I was elevated to a different status, burdened only with the usual stereotypes that are used to characterise Americans abroad.

And yet my British 'sister' and I were still bound, superficially by our skin colour, and historically by a legacy of similar oppression. It was from these early subtle intimations that I first began to understand the full magnitude and *universality* of the 'race problem' – that common experience of racial discrimination, prejudice, hatred and exploitation that binds together people of colour all around the world. My own identity, the person I felt myself to be, was redefined in relation to this sense of an intrinsic link with the global experience of racism. It became important for me to explore more fully the implications of this revelation and I saw my academic studies as the perfect opportunity to do just that.

Black Tribunes is the culmination of more than five years of primary and secondary research on the topic of black political participation and representation in Britain. A substantial portion of the material was first submitted as a thesis for a master's degree in politics from Oxford in 1988. In 1990, I subsequently took one year from my studies at Harvard Law School to write, revise and update this work for publication.

While my interest in the subject of black Britons was initially sparked by the similarities between the American and British experience, in the process of researching and writing this book, I have also come to realise, and respect more fully, the differences. My thoughts on the subject have evolved with the help of many people. I benefitted greatly from the early supervision of my Oxford tutors Jim Sharpe and Marian FitzGerald.

My field research was made possible by the financial contribution of the British Council and by numerous individuals I interviewed who gave so freely of their time and expertise. I would like to give particular acknowledgement to Bernie Grant, Lord Pitt of Hampstead and Paul Boateng, who took special interest in my research and made efforts to help me contact activists. A special thanks to Paul for his thoughtful comments in the foreword to this book, and to his family who so generously became my family away from home.

In the course of this project I have been encouraged and sustained by a group of terrific friends in England and back home. Although the list is too long, I hope it will suffice to say that I am deeply indebted to you all. But special thanks to Allison, my best friend who stood by me in my decision to take a year off from Harvard Law School, and to Tunde and Tselane who filled that year with laughter.

Finally, I would like to extend my heartfelt gratitude to the staff at Lawrence & Wishart. But above all, thanks to my family – Mom, Dad, Andrew and Anthony – who were a constant source of inspiration, even at a distance.

Foreword

Paul Boateng

Terri Sewell's intelligent and comprehensive study of the issue of race and representation in Britain provides some challenging insights into contemporary British politics and the developing role of black people in it.

Contrary to popular wisdom, there is nothing new about black participation in British politics. Our history and experience as black people, and our contribution to the building of this society, are denied here as in so much else. The black strand is in fact woven into the weft and warp of British political history. William Davidson, of Jamaican origin, was one of the Cato Street conspirators executed in 1820 for allegedly plotting to blow up the House of Commons. Robert Wedderburn, Jamaican by birth, was prominent in the Society of Spencean Philanthropists in 1817, regularly drew crowds of 200 and more to his meetings in Soho and was imprisoned for sedition variously at Newgate and Carlisle. William Cuffay, born in Britain of African origin, was one of the principal leaders of the Chartist movement, the first mass political movement of the British working class. His election in 1842 as President of London's Metropolitan Delegate Council led to a lampoon in the satirical magazine *Punch*, depicting him and London's Chartists as the 'black man and his party'. This finds a ready echo in the contemporary press.

The late nineteenth and early twentieth centuries saw the election at various times of three MPs of Indian origin, Dadabhia Naoroji, Sir M.M. Bhownagree and Shapurji Saklatvala. These represented a diversity of political opinion, Liberal centrist, Conservative and Communist respectively, and – despite attacks that centred on their race as much as their politics – made an impact in the House of Commons and on the politics of their time.

Saklatvala, with his friend and colleague J.R. Arthur, Pan-Africanist and first black mayor of Battersea in 1912, made real the links between the struggle for peace and social justice of the peoples of Britain and the Third World. These, our predecessors, whilst never denying their race and the responsibilities which that brought with it, never allowed themselves or their political contribution to be circumscribed by the colour of their skin.

The divide between those who define themselves and their politics only by their pigmentation, and those who demand for themselves and for black people in general the right not to be labelled and marginalised by race, is a real and continuing one. Terri Sewell casts much light on the form that the argument which surrounds these positions has taken in present–day Britain. The arguments are important ones and cannot be swept under the carpet. It is a matter of deep regret, however, that sectarianism and the politics of personality have made the divide between these two opposing approaches to politics a yawning chasm in which the everyday issues that confront the community, and the need for a relevant political agenda for economic and social emancipation, are often lost. We must seek to bridge that divide, or at the very least co-exist and co-operate, if the real gains that have been made in recent years are to be consolidated and bear fruit.

The black community, and the African, Caribbean and Asian cultures that go to make it up, present a dynamic and vibrant force. Black Britons increasingly reject the notion simply of survival and seek instead success in a society where racial disadvantage and discrimination remain a continuing fact of life. They demand – and create themselves – strategies for change. The youth on the streets of Brixton, Southall, Moss Side and Toxteth, have shown only too clearly that they will not accept marginalisation. Come what may, blacks in Britain are here to stay. The 1990s are a new decade, and as the great jazz tune goes, 'There'll be some changes made'.

Paul Boateng, MP
House of Commons, Westminster

1   Race and the British Political Context

We have won a great victory here tonight ... For 400 years we have waited to go to that place of our independence and I say this, we went before as humble petitioners – Never again! We go now as Socialist Tribunes of all the people, black and white.

Paul Boateng, MP
Election Night Speech
Brent Town Hall
11 June 1987

On 11 June 1987 four black MPs were elected to the British Parliament. Their election represented a watershed in the politics of race in Britain. Prior to the June 1987 election, there had *never* been an African or Afro-Caribbean member of the 650-seat British Parliament. Although three Asians were elected in the late nineteenth and early twentieth century, this recent victory constituted the first non-white presence in Westminster since the Communist Shapurji Saklatvala won the seat of Battersea North in 1924.[1] The election of Labour candidates, Paul Boateng for Brent South, Bernie Grant for Tottenham, Diane Abbott for Hackney North/Stoke Newington and Keith Vaz for Leicester East marked a major development for ethnic minority representation in British politics. Paul Boateng's dramatic emphasis on the historic significance of the 1987 electoral victories expressed the sentiments of many of Britain's most powerless peoples, that indeed their time had finally come.

This electoral success in fact represented several years of intense

13

political effort and, at times, controversy: the 1980s ushered in a new era for black politics in Britain in which black *representation* was placed on the mainstream political agenda for the first time. Great advances were made, especially on the local level which witnessed a phenomenal rise in the number of black councillors. For example, in the 1977 County Council elections, there were just 37 black candidates of whom four were elected. Yet by 1983, in a comparatively small town like Luton, thirteen black candidates were elected. Naturally enough, the growth in representation was particularly evident in urban areas of high black population. In the Greater London area, for example, 67 black Labour councillors were elected in May 1982 and in four years time that number had risen to 80, plus five Conservative black councillors and two Liberals.[2] Increasingly, black people aspired and were elected to leadership positions within local government. In 1984, Bernie Grant became the first black council leader in Britain for the Labour council in Haringey, north London. His success was followed in 1986 by the election of Merle Amory and Linda Bellos as council leaders for Brent and Lambeth respectively. Also in the same year, councillor Mohammed Ajeeb was elected the first Asian Lord Mayor in Britain for Bradford.

While the growth in the 1980s of the numbers of black local councillors was encouraging, its impact was nevertheless tempered by the realisation that in actuality there were only about 150 black councillors out of an estimated total of 25,000 local council seats.[3] Coupled with this relatively low percentage is the fact that black representation was not evenly distributed but heavily skewed towards urban areas with well over half of the black local councillors in the Greater London area. Still, the 1980s saw a rise in the number of black parliamentary candidates from five in the 1979 general election, to 18 in the 1983 election, to 27 black candidates in the 1987 election. Although these figures represent a very small increase given the total number of seats available, their significance lies in the extent to which they were an indication of a new development in the politics of race in Britain. The electoral challenges and successes of black people in the 1980s indicated both a strategic change in the way black people approached the British political system and a change in the way the political system dealt with their presence.

Black Presence in Britain[4]

Many misconceptions surround the presence of black people in Britain. One of the most prevalent is the belief that the emergence of black communities is a very recent development in British history. It is argued that the relative 'novelty' of black people in Britain results in a lack of experience within the political system and is, therefore, the major cause for their under-representation. According to the logic of this argument, black political success will eventually occur after black people become familiar with the workings of the political system and more integrated into British society in general. Although most people associate the presence of black people with postwar migration and the arrival of the *Empire Windrush* in 1948, the reality is that there have been black people in Britain for almost 500 years. Several political observers and historians have gone into great depth to document the existence of black people throughout British history: Peter Fryer, in his *Staying Power*, provides evidence that black people have been born in Britain since 1505.[5] Not only was there a black presence but a sizeable population was recorded as far back as the eighteenth century. Then, as now, black communities were heavily concentrated in urban areas. As early as 1761, some 14,000 to 20,000 black people were reportedly living in London alone.

Mass migration of black people to Britain, however, was induced and nurtured by the postwar conditions of the late 1940s and early 1950s. One of the most dramatic, though unexpected, political effects for Britain of World War II was the large-scale settlement of hundreds of thousands of people from the New Commonwealth countries and Pakistan (NCWP). Economic and social conditions within many Commonwealth countries, especially in the West Indies which made up the first wave of migrants, were sufficiently harsh to 'push' many black people to leave in search of a better life. Operating simultaneously were the 'pull' factors of employment vacancies, improved life chances and the prospect of the higher standard of living which existed in Britain at the time.[6] Such opportunities seemed like a pot of gold at the end of a rainbow to many migrants, luring them towards a land of potential hope and glory.

The number of Commonwealth immigrants more than doubled

in 1951-61 from 256,000 to 541,000.[7] The economic boom and the
ensuing labour shortage which occurred after the Second World
War served as the main stimulus for migration. But the effect of the
overt and direct recruitment of black people by the British
government should not be underestimated. Black people in the
Caribbean were openly encouraged to emigrate: official notices,
posters, and advertisements in local papers in the Caribbean
enticed many with the promise of jobs and better opportunities in
Britain. They came as manual workers, willing and able to accept
the low status jobs that white workers refused. As dustmen,
postmen, transport workers and nurses, black people became
disproportionately represented in the British working class and
their employment was most heavily concentrated in the public
sector. Official British encouragement was not fuelled by some
liberal-minded or paternalistic desire for cultural diversity, but
rather by the sheer necessity for additional labour to rebuild a
war-torn economy. But while the heads of state acknowledged the
economic priority, the average British citizen neither wanted nor
understood the need for change.

The black migrants were met with much hostility. White workers
feared displacement and competition, while the white elite felt
threatened by the encroaching threat to a mythical 'English way of
life'. The legacies of Empire and colonialism had devastating effects
on the relationship between blacks and whites, influencing the
expectations and aspirations of both communities.

As members (or former members) of the decaying British
Empire, most black people arrived carrying British citizenship
passports – under the terms of the 1948 Nationality Act, they could
hold either UK or Commonwealth passports – and rightfully
expecting all the amenities and rights due them as subjects of the
Crown. Many black men and women from the Caribbean had
served as soldiers and auxiliaries in the war and had paid their dues
– fighting for 'King and country'. Racial hatred and *unequal*
opportunities were the thanks they received for believing that they
too were included in the notion of 'Commonwealth'. The British
polity was torn between upholding the comparatively liberal ideals
of Empire and accommodating the reality of widespread public
resentment and hostility towards black people.

The net result of the mass migration of the 1950s and 1960s was to place enormous pressure on British policy-makers to change their policy on immigration. Gone were the days of '*Civis Britannicus Sum*' when in 1954 Henry Hopkinson, then Minister of State for the Colonies, could righteously proclaim, 'whatever his colour may be, we take pride in the fact that he wants to and can come to the mother country'.[8] As the number of immigrants increased and the public hostility mounted, the 'open door' policy of the Commonwealth ideal was ended.

People of ethnic minority origin presently consitute about five per cent of the total UK population of 55 million. There are an estimated 2.6 million ethnic minority citizens living in Britain. The category of 'black' contains many sub-divisions and is most often defined by its two largest groups: Afro-Caribbean and Asian. Asians of Indian subcontinent origin make up 52 per cent (1.3 million) of the non-white population while Afro-Caribbeans constitute 24 per cent (0.56 million); those of mixed descent constitute 0.5 million (11%) and the remaining 13 per cent comprises minorities from South-East Asia, the Mediterranean and other parts of the New Commonwealth.[9] Although a 1984 study predicted that the number of black people will increase to 3.3 million by the end of this century, they will still only constitute 6.7 per cent of the population.[10]

Many commentators point to this relatively small percentage of ethnic minorities as the most compelling reason for black under-representation in the political system. It is argued that if black people made up a more substantial voting bloc, then their demands for greater political participation would be answered. This forms yet another common misconception that only through an absolute increase in the overall number of black people can electoral success be achieved. This view totally overlooks the importance of the large numbers of black people within certain parliamentary constituencies. While black people comprise a small percentage of the overall British population, they are highly concentrated in metropolitan areas and command a substantial voting bloc in those areas. Approximately 70 per cent of the non-white population in Britain lives in metropolitan areas, compared with only 30 per cent of the white population. 41 per cent of all black people live in London alone.[11]

The five per cent figure, therefore, is misleading because what really matters in British politics is the population within constituencies. There are an estimated 60 parliamentary seats where the NCWP population is at least fifteen per cent, as Table 1.1 shows.

Table 1.1

Ethnic minority population
in selected parliamentary constituencies

CONSTITUENCY	1981 census %	1987 (estimates) %
Brent South	45.7	55.6
Ealing Southall	43.7	53.2
Birmingham Ladywood	42.8	52.0
Birmingham Small Heath	38.8	46.8
Tottenham	37.5	45.3
Birmingham Sparkbrook	35.2	42.5
Newham North-West	32.7	39.3
Newham North-East	32.6	39.3
Hackney North & Stoke Newington	30.7	37.0
Brent East	29.9	36.6
Bradford West	27.0	32.5
Leyton	26.7	32.2
Leicester East	26.3	31.7
Leicester South	25.3	30.5
Vauxhall	25.1	30.3
Bethnal Green and Stepney	24.4	29.4
Hackney South & Shoreditch	24.4	29.4
Tooting	24.1	29.3
Norwood	23.4	28.3
Lewisham Deptford	23.4	28.2
Brent North	23.0	27.8
Croydon North-West	22.7	27.3
Battersea	21.6	26.0
Hornsey and Wood Green	21.3	25.7
Warley East	21.2	25.6
Islington North	21.0	25.4
Slough	20.9	25.4
Peckham	20.6	24.8
Streatham	20.2	24.6
Ilford South	19.9	24.0
Feltham and Heston	19.6	23.6
Walthamstow	19.6	23.6
Hammersmith	18.2	22.0
Enfield Southgate	18.1	21.8

CONSTITUENCY	1981 census %	1987 (estimates) %
Wolverhampton South-East	17.9	21.7
Wolverhampton South-West	17.7	21.6
Derby South	17.3	20.8
Stretford	17.2	20.7
Dulwich	17.2	20.7
Edmonton	17.0	20.5
Harrow East	16.9	20.3
Finchley	16.4	20.0
Coventry North-East	16.3	20.0
Birmingham Perry Barr	16.0	19.3
Luton South	16.0	19.3
Bow and Poplar	15.4	18.5
Walsall South	15.1	18.2
Westminster North	15.0	18.2
Bradford North	15.0	18.1
Blackburn	14.8	17.9
Hendon South	14.8	17.8
Huddersfield	14.7	17.7
Ealing North	14.3	17.2
Ealing Acton	14.0	17.9
Brentford and Isleworth	13.7	16.5
Croydon North-East	13.4	16.1
Harrow West	13.3	16.0
Newham South	13.0	15.7
Manchester Gorton	12.4	15.0
Leicester West	12.3	15.0

Source: Muhammad Anwar, *Race and Politics*, Tavistock Publications, London 1986, p165-6.

On average, the percentage of black people in the most heavily non-white constituencies is about 30 per cent and should indicate sufficient electoral presence to exert palpable political pressure in those constituencies. The fact that blacks wield relatively little political power within most of these constituencies suggests that many more forces are operating which militate against the strength of sheer numbers.[12]

Changing patterns of black political participation

One of the most significant developments affecting black political participation has been the change in black attitudes and approaches to the political system. During the 1950s and 1960s, the predominant attitude of black people towards the political establishment could be characterised as 'tacit acceptance'. The majority of the black migrants came to Britain for economic reasons, in search of a better life for themselves and their families. Not all came, however, with the intention of staying. The most common scenario was one of a migrant worker leaving behind his/her family with the hope of making enough money to return and make life better for the family back home. Many intended to work, study and then go home after a few years of prosperity.

Black people came with grand illusions about what life in Britain would offer them. What they found was a society pervaded with racism, induced by the colonial legacy. They were shocked by and unprepared for the overt, and covert, racism that confronted them in Britain. During these initial years, black people did not actively pursue redress for their experience of racism through formal political means. On the contrary, most people, unconsciously if not consciously, adopted a 'bear with it' attitude towards the blatant discrimination they encountered. Perseverance was considered the greatest virtue. Since few intended to stay in Britain more than a couple of years, most did not seek change through participation in the system. They were prepared tacitly to accept their abhorrent and unequal condition as only temporary. Most black people felt they had little stake in a system that they would only be a part of for a relatively short time.

Some black people, however, did see the need for political action and became actively involved in politics, seeing the left as their natural ally. Joining the Labour Party and also the Communist Party (in the early 1950s), these black activists tended to emphasise the importance of equal rights within the workforce and community. They very rarely developed a separate black politics. Since the labour movement by and large paid only lip service to questions of equal rights, black activists made little progress in these organisations. Although the labour movement had a rhetoric of anti-discrimination, black people found it difficult to make their voices heard.

The difficulties of organisation, combined with the 'tacit acceptance' approach adopted by the silent majority of black people, has been a major impediment to black political progress in Britain. As long as black people placed no special demands on the system, the system made no efforts to accommodate them. It was only with a decisive change in perceptions and approach that black people began to achieve relative success.

The 1962 Commonwealth Immigrants Act was an official acknowledgement of the perceived threat posed by black people. It signalled the start of a tightening of immigration controls. The myth of 'returning back home' also began to fade as more black migrants became dependent on their way of life in Britain for financial support, and family ties and other relationships made the prospect of leaving a difficult one. As the British government got tougher with each successive passage of anti-immigration legislation, so too did black people become more defensive of their political and civil rights.

Encouraged by the momentum of the civil rights movement developing in America, black Britons tried their own hand at organisation by forming the Campaign Against Racial Discrimination (CARD) in the late 1960s (see chapter 2). Though the success of CARD was short-lived, its significance lay in the desire of black people to mobilise and make demands on the political institution.

The 1970s witnessed a further breakdown in the willingness of black people to accept the inequality of their treatment. Throughout this decade black Britons began to develop their own forms of cultural expression: the Notting Hill Carnival is a vivid example. Under the influence of black American political development, black people became increasingly willing to confront white people with their 'differentness'. One political observer suggests that the presence of black people has evolved over three distinct phases and dates them specifically:

The first, from the fifties to 1962, was dominated by the ideology of assimilation or integration. This meant one thing to the establishment and quite another to us. The second, from 1962 to 1976, was characterised by the phrase 'cultural diversity', which represented the state's retreat from a kind of integration that was phoney in the first place, but which it pretended to strengthen by supporting – up to a point – the black community's assertion of its cultural identity in a hostile environment. The third phase, which is still being played out in the eighties, is one where the agenda is finally being acknowledged as having been defined by the black community itself: the fight for equality.[13]

Whether or not the distinctions are as clear-cut as denoted, it is increasingly clear that the 1980s did mark a new era of black political activism in Britain. Their antagonism was unashamedly directed at the British political establishment as they actively sought to voice their indignation at the current inequities. The 'direct confrontation' approach took several forms – informally in urban unrest, and formally in intensified political activism at both grassroots and institutional levels.

The extent to which black activists were successful was, and still is, largely determined by the extent to which the system has allowed them to succeed. By 'system' I do not mean some conspiratorial organ of class rule ('the Establishment' perhaps), but the complex lattice of governmental institutions, local and national administrative units, party political structures, professions, associations and cultures that make up the British system of parliamentary democracy. While black people at many times have not promoted their own interests, the British political system has not exactly facilitated their transition from powerlessness to empowerment.

The British Polity's Approaches to Race Relations

The era from postwar migration to the passage of the Commonwealth Immigrants Act of 1962 was characterised by what can best be described as 'benign neglect'. There was a conscious effort made by all the political parties to keep race out of politics as much as possible:

> Any discussion of immigration and race relations, any suggestion that they were legitimate and important subjects for political debate, was frowned on. It was as though no one could talk about immigration control without being racist. This strategy may not have amounted to a conspiracy but it did indicate a common inclination, shared by most members of the upper and middle classes of British institutions, towards keeping Britain 'civilised' in racial matters.[14]

The 'tacit acceptance' attitude of blacks themselves, which corresponded to this period, made it possible to maintain a continuity of the consensus on race for almost two decades. Successive governments, Labour and Conservative, sought to defuse the issue. In retrospect, the continuity achieved was astounding.

It was the anti-black riots of 1958, combined with the growing numbers of immigrants, that struck a major blow to consensus politics. The hostility and resentment of whites, which were the chief cause of the Nottingham and Notting Hill riots of 1958, demonstrated the real extent to which racism pervaded British society. Racial issues could no longer be avoided. The government's response was the Commonwealth Immigrants Act of 1962, which marked an end to the 'laissez-faire' strategy of the 1950s.[15]

The politics of race entered a new phase after 1962. Bi-partisan consensus began to revolve around the necessity for control, operating on several levels. Control, in the external sense, describes in fact the efforts to limit the number of immigrants. In this regard, the Commonwealth Immigrants Act of 1962 marked an official slamming of the 'open door', which had been the policy of the old Empire. Previously all United Kingdom subjects, whether citizens of the Commonwealth or the United Kingdom, had been free to enter or leave the 'motherland'.

In another way, the government strove to control racial issues by distancing itself from the impact of its policies. Prompted to provide official legislation, the government sought to contain the issue by placing it on the periphery of its administrative responsibility. It was this 'peripheralisation of race' which became the next major development: the object of the government was to maintain relative autonomy from race problems.[16]

When race 'problems' were addressed there was a concerted effort to decentralise the issue. The potential embarrassment to the governing classes of incidents such as the election victory for the racist Tory Peter Griffiths in Smethwick in the general election of 1964, the overwhelming reception given to Enoch Powell's 'rivers of blood' speech in 1968, and the rise of the National Front, reaffirmed the need to shift the responsibility of racial issues away from central government. By delegating race problems to local authorities and 'quasi-autonomous non-governmental organisations' (quangos), the government removed itself from any unpleasant consequences produced by its policies. 'The management of race politics must rank as one of the great political 'jobs' of the 20th century', Jim Bulpitt asserts in his article, 'Continuity, Autonomy and Peripheralisation'. 'The interests of the centre were satisfied.

The interests of blacks and whites on the periphery were left to chance.'[17] Thus the question of race was kept off the mainstream national agenda for four decades, for twenty years through the operation of a *laissez-faire* policy, and for a further twenty by an attempt to treat issues of race as questions for the 'local community'. The handling of racial issues over the past four decades was characterised therefore, despite numerous changes of government, by its extraordinary consistency. This continuity could only have been maintained by a successful bi-partisan consensus, manifesting itself in the policy of peripheralisation or 'diminished responsibility' as it might be termed.

The 1980s, however, witnessed a new phase of activism by black people and enhanced responsiveness on the part of the political parties. Interest from the political parties came initially in response to a report published by the Community Relations Commission after the two general elections of 1974 which drew attention to the importance of the 'black vote'.[18] These findings, discussed more fully in subsequent chapters, were very significant in contributing to the political climate of the early 1980s. The consciousness-raising effect of the riots in 1981 (largely via the subsequent report by Lord Scarman), and the campaign for black sections in the Labour Party (see chapter 5), also had a profound impact. It came to be perceived by political parties that black people might be of use to them in some seats, and there was also an establishment recognition that the complete marginalisation of black people from the political mainstream could lead to black disaffection – which could be dangerous. It was the Home Affairs Select Committee in its Racial Disadvantage report in 1981 that finally admitted: 'It is by successful participation in the political system rather than through separation or special representation that the political future of Britain's ethnic minorities must lie.'[19] The new activism by black people and this corresponding responsiveness of the British polity was crucial for the political advances made by blacks in the 1980s.

Just how long would this revised attitude on the part of the British polity last? The very nature and structure of the British political system with its emphasis on class loyalties militates against the successful participation of black people in politics. The most significant recurring factor in the political predicament of black Britons is the conflict between class and race.

The Primacy of Class

The primacy of class has had major implications for black political participation and representation in Britain. While there are other factors that contribute to party allegiance, class has traditionally been the most decisive influence. In politics, class allegiance has *traditionally* translated into the upper and middle classes affiliating to the Conservative Party and a working-class affiliation to the Labour Party, although this picture has never been as comprehensive as has at times been suggested: there has always been a minority, but latterly significant, working-class Tory constituency. In general, however, both major parties have, in both ideology and image, appealed to their respective 'natural' class. The Labour Party, in particular, was decisively born out of the labour movement. Because most black people are working class, they have associated themselves (actively and passively) with the Labour Party. And the class-based nature of the British political system itself has historically placed the pressure of answering black political demands squarely on the shoulders of the Labour Party. The other parties until quite recently showed no desire and felt little need to woo the black electorate. In many ways, as this book will explore in later chapters, the future of black people in politics is directly connected to the future of the Labour Party.

Although it is important to acknowledge the recent trends towards both realignment of class allegiance and dealignment from any political allegiance, the core electoral support of each of the parties is still its traditional class base. Anthony Heath, Roger Jowell and John Curtice in their book, *How Britain Votes*, challenge contemporary thinking and argue that class has not lost its pre-eminence as an explanation for political loyalties. What they argue is that the decline in class voting has been *relative* not absolute:

> Contemporary accounts of the decline of class are no more plausible than those of the 1950s. The commentators have once again confused a decline in *overall* support for Labour with decline in its *relative* class support ... Labour remained a class party in 1983; it was simply a less successful class party than before.[20]

This is of crucial significance to the Labour Party which has been disproportionately affected by the decline in class-determined voting. What the relative versus absolute argument implies is that class allegiance is based on something more than just voting strength. Despite actual electoral performance, the British party system is still perceived as class-based, regardless of whether people themselves support the party of their 'opposite' class. Labour's apparent decline can be attributed to the Conservatives' success in appealing to voters outside their core middle- and upper-class constituency.

It is the public image and perception of parties that maintains the class-based nature of the British political culture. Image is an especially important factor for the Labour Party. It has the difficult task of retaining its working class support whilst trying to deny that it is a class party. Part of the solution to this problem is to replace class with a notion of an appeal to 'the people'. But conceptions of 'the people' remain homogeneous. 'The people' or 'working people' are not broken down into different constituencies, with possible conflicting interests. It is this self-defined image which inhibits it from acknowledging distinctions along racial lines. This is precisely the problem which confronted Labour in the battle over black sections within the Party. Its dominant ethos of representing all working-class interests regardless of vertical distinctions like gender and race, inhibits the Labour Party from accepting the demands for a separate entity based on race. Black activists, however, point to the existence of women's sections and youth sections as a contradiction in this logic. Although this is the topic of another chapter, the controversy over black sections does outline the nature of the conflict blacks encounter when they seek to participate in a class-based system.

The very nature of the British polity, with the continuing importance of class within it, militates against black electoral success. The primacy of class has kept race out of the political arena. For several decades, there was a bi-partisan consensus to minimise the impact of race on party politics. Racial issues, such as immigration, were avoided at all costs. Black demands were addressed in the context of the working class struggle and had very little legitimacy as issues in and of themselves. The primacy of class, Zig Layton-Henry in *Race, Government and Politics in Britain* states, is one of the key reasons why race was seldom seen as a source of legitimate political action:

> This reluctance to focus on race as a source of political action and conflict was reinforced by two factors: first, a belief in the primacy of class as the basic concept for analysing political behaviour and decision making, and secondly, a feeling that racism was both irrational and immoral and therefore distinctions based on race should not be given credence by using 'race' as a category of political analysis.[21]

This, then, is the context for black people's participation in the British body politic.

Notes

1. Three MPs from the Indian subcontinent (all Parsees) were elected to the House of Commons before the Second World War. Dadabhai Naoroji was the first elected in 1892 for the Liberal Party with a majority of five at Finsbury Central. The second was Sir Mancherjee Bhownagree who was elected twice as a Conservative for the seat of Bethnal Green North East in 1895 and 1900. The third was Shapurji Saklatvala who was also twice elected for Battersea North, as a Labour candidate in 1922 and for the Communist Party in 1924. In the House of Lords, there was also one member from the Indian subcontinent, Lord Sinha of Raijpur who served from 1863-1928. After the Second World War there were no black MPs, although there were three black members of the House of Lords – Lords Constantine, Pitt and Chitnis.

2. Zig Layton-Henry and Donley T. Studlar, 'The Electoral participation of Blacks and Asians: Integration or Alienation?', *Parliamentary Affairs*, Summer 1985, pp.312-4.

3. *Ibid.*

4. For the purposes of this book the term 'black' will denote peoples of both Afro-Caribbean and Indian subcontinental origin. Census and statistical information most often defines 'black' as people from the New Commonwealth Countries and Pakistan (NCWP). While there are many problems with the use of NCWP in defining black people, it is generally used in mainstream political discourse. Thus, throughout this work, 'black' will refer to both Afro-Caribbeans and Asians collectively, unless differentiations between the groups are expressly made.

5. Peter Fryer, *Staying Power: The History of Black People in Britain*, Pluto Press, London 1984, p.xi.

6. Zig Layton-Henry, *The Politics of Race*, George Allen & Unwin, London 1984, p.17.

7. Muhammad Anwar, *Race and Politics*, Tavistock Publications, London 1986, p.8.

8. Anwar, *op. cit.*, p.8.

9. *Ibid*, p.10-11.

10. Jim Bulpitt, 'Continuity, Autonomy and Peripheralisation', in Leyton-Henry and Rich (eds), *Race, Government and Politics in Britain*, Macmillan, London 1986, p.19.

11. Colin Brown, *Black and White Britain: The Third PSI Survey*, Policy Studies Institute, London 1984.

12. Marian FitzGerald, *Political Parties and Black People*, Runnymede Trust, London 1984, p.10.

13. Trevor Carter, *Shattering Illusions: West Indians in British Politics*, Lawrence & Wishart, London 1986, p.14.

14. Bulpitt, *op. cit.*, p.28.

15. *Ibid.*, p.27.

16. *Ibid.*, p.23.

17. *Ibid.*, p.23.

18. Community Relations Commission, 'Participation of Ethnic Minorities in the General Election, October 1974', 1975. See also Marian FitzGerald, *Political Parties and Black People*, Runnymede Trust, London 1984.

19. Home Affairs Select Committee, *Racial Disadvantages*, HMSO, London 1981, paragraph 76.

20. Anthony Heath, Roger Jowell and John Curtice, *How Britain Votes*, Pergamon Press, Oxford 1985, p.29.

21. Layton-Henry, *Race, Government, and Politics in Britain*, Macmillan, London 1986, p.3.

2 Between the Mainstream and the Margins

> The fact is that blacks have only really survived socially and politically in this society over the past 20 years precisely through developing their own politics of resistance. They've had very little help from the traditional political organisations. And what they say is that working in these organisations is a kind of deviation from the real task. We'll get lost inside the parliamentary mechanism, they say, and black politics will be confined – becoming just one more issue in the many on Labour's agenda.[1]
>
> – Stuart Hall

In spite of the unpromising terrain, recent years have seen considerable growth in formal black involvement in the mainstream of British politics, through their participation in elections and such established political institutions as parties, trade unions and lobbying or pressure groups. However, black people also have a long history of political activism through less formal means of direct action and protest. This chapter chronicles the nature and viability of both mainstream and grassroots forms of political participation and assesses their effectiveness in developing a strategy for black political empowerment in Britain.

The political participation of groups in the mainstream of political institutions is often regarded as a gauge for the resolve and vigour of those seeking political redress for grievances. Rightly or not, mainstream political participation is the most 'acceptable' means by which problems are solved and interests are promoted in the political arena. But mere participation in the political system has never meant, nor translated into, equal access to the decision-making or agenda-setting processes. The representative nature of western democracies like Britain ensures a hierarchy of power and privilege such that only a few have such access.

The incorporation of disparate groups into the political system has occurred unevenly and, for black people especially, unequally. Their capacity to influence political outcomes has been severely limited by their lack of political resources with which to gain access to the appropriate channels. Some would argue that black people have been systematically excluded from full political integration, while others maintain that they have become disillusioned and therefore alienated themselves from participation. Although some black activists do participate eagerly in party politics, the vast majority of black people, like white people, are simply not involved in politics. The extent, if any, to which most people, irrespective of colour, commit themselves politically is usually in the form of a political identification which may or may not translate into voting on election day. Therefore, while most black Britons have identified most closely with the Labour Party, their identification has not necessarily nor directly transformed into Party membership. This fact, in and of itself, is not surprising considering that only five per cent of the British population are actually members of political parties.[2]

Most black activists have been disillusioned by the committe-ridden bureaucracy involved in mainstream politics and have little confidence in the effectiveness of political parties to bring about change, especially on issues of racial discrimination which have all too often been regulated to agencies on the periphery (see chapter 1). Party politics is specifically bound by complex rules, regulations and a convoluted system of patronage. Political parties' basic *raison d'être* is to secure power, and pandering to minority concerns has never been perceived as electorally expedient. Consequently, black people have only survived politically over the years by cultivating their own forms of political empowerment through community activism. Black politics in its 'purest' form – meaning the setting of the political agenda by black people on black concerns – is never likely to be wholly reconciled with mainstream party politics. In the British experience, this means that black politics is blocked, redefined and diluted to fit, if at all, with the political priorities of the Labour Party.

Black people are not alone in their lack of interest in political parties. Many white Britons also share the same apathy. This lack of confidence has been reflected in a loss of faith in the efficacy of voting. A 1984 GLC report confirms this observation. When questioned as to the best way to 'influence government', membership in a political party was seen as effective by only 5 per cent of whites and Afro-Caribbeans, though twice as many Asian respondents mentioned it.[3] When given the choice of 'voting, lobbying or pressure group/campaigning' as ways of influencing government, voting was not seen as the best method by the majority of the respondents. Table 2.1 shows that Afro-Caribbeans place the least emphasis on voting and see campaigning and pressure group activities as the most effective way to influence government. White respondents preferred lobbying, while Asians were the only group to consider voting as the most effective means of effecting change.

Table 2.1
Preferred Ways of Influencing Government by Ethnic Group

	Afro-Caribbeans	Asians	Whites
Voting	15%	30%	26%
Pressure Group/ Campaigning	34%	21%	23%
Lobbying	24%	17%	28%

*Base: All of those naming at least one way of influencing government.
Source: Greater London Council, Survey of Political Activity and Attitudes to Race Relations, 1985.

This survey points out the divergence that exists within the black communities regarding modes of political participation. Asians and Afro-Caribbeans differ, often sharply, in their political behaviour. The Asian community tends to show a greater propensity to participate in mainstream politics. Unlike Afro-Caribbeans, they tend to take this more seriously as one of their 'civic duties'. Research confirms that Asians vote more than Afro-Caribbeans, and also suggests that they have a higher turn-out rate proportionately than even their white neighbours in certain wards.[4] British Asians are committed voters but seem, as a group, less willing to be engaged in explicitly political activities. Layton-Henry and Studlar observed the irony in black voting:

> We are faced with the paradox that the group least likely to vote [West Indians] participate more than whites and Asians in these other respects [political activities other than voting] ... In each instance it is the blacks who are more likely to participate. The evidence thus suggests that Asians in Britain form a relatively apolitical but voting part of the electorate while blacks are more interested in politics generally but put relatively little value on voting. Particularly when political activities involve direct political discussion and open commitment, Asians seem less willing to become involved than either blacks or whites.[5]

The picture that emerges is one of a heterogeneous black community which shares a common enemy, namely racism, but that varies in its approach to dealing with the problem. In the most general terms, Afro-Caribbeans have tended to be more prepared to confront and defy the discriminatory practices of state institutions, while British Asians have sought largely to working within established norms.

In recent times, however, this gap in modes of political expression between Asian and Afro-Caribbean communities has narrowed. The advent of the Salman Rushdie Affair has 'politicised' Asians as no other issue since formal mass immigration ceased to be a national concern. The controversy surrounding the publication of *The Satanic Verses* has mobilised British Muslims into intensive extra-parliamentary activities. The rallies and protests in areas with high Asian Muslim populations and the open endorsement and active participation in bookburning suggested the potential strength of Asians as a political force to be reckoned with. The extent of their religious and moral outrage lead also to the formation in 1989 of a separate and independent extremist political party, the Islamic Party, which fielded candidates in the May 1990 local elections, although with little success.

Factors Affecting Participation

The experience of black political participation in Britain has been defined and limited by the tremendous impediments that stand in the way of their progress. Any talk of black political integration must take into account the structural, cultural and organisational factors which undermine their influence.

The demography of the black British population has important implications for the nature and effectiveness of black political participation. The fact, as discussed earlier, of the relatively small size of the black population is indeed a large problem affecting the potential strength of black mobilisation. But also significant for the lack of black representation within political parties is the fact that the black population is disproportionately young. In other words, large segments of the community are below the voting age. A 1984 Policy Studies Institute (PSI) report found that half of the West Indian and Asian population was under 25 years of age, while only 35 per cent of the general population was that young. The Asian population was the youngest with 40 per cent of its members under the age of 16, as compared with 30 per cent of West Indians and only 22 per cent of the general population that age.[6] Today, the age structure reflects a greater number of blacks than whites amongst first-time voters. As Table 2.2 illustrates, an average of 26 per cent of the black population are between the 16-29 age group, while only 22 per cent of the white population are within that age group.

Table 2.2
Age Structure of Ethnic Groups (%)

	under 16	16-29	30-44	45-64 men 45-59 women	65+men 60+women
Whites	20	22	20	19	19
West Indian	25	33	15	22	*
Indian	31	27	24	14	*
Pakistani	43	25	18	13	*
Bangladeshi	50	21	14	14	*

* indicates numbers too small to be accurately expressed as %
Source: Labour Force Surveys, 1985-87.

Even as the black population matures, other demographic factors such as their low socio-economic status will still dramatically affect their political involvement and the kinds of political resources they have at their disposal. Politics is a luxury that most black people simply cannot afford. Aside from being young, the black population is also disproportionately working class, unskilled and under-educated. In 1984, 83 per cent of West Indian men and 73 per cent of Asian men were in manual jobs, compared with 58 per cent of whites. The disparity was even more dramatic in the top socio-economic category, where 19 per cent of whites were in professional and managerial occupations, compared to 13 per cent of Asians and only 5 per cent of West Indians.[7]

Socio-economic status (SES) has an enormous bearing on political opportunity and resources. The theory that low SES hampers political participation is now well documented:

> Research ... shows over and over again that in modern industrial societies, people of lower socio-economic status have fewer political resources than people of higher status, they generally join fewer organisations, are less likely to rise to leadership positions with those organisations, and the higher the office the less likely they are to fill it.[8]

The Labour Force Survey of 1985-87 gives further evidence. Of all males over 16, 43 per cent of the West Indian men had no qualifications, 41 per cent of the Indian men and 37 per cent of the whites, while a substantial 68 per cent of the Pakistani and Bangladeshi men had no educational qualifications.

There is also considerable disparity between and within different ethnic minority communities. Although there are inconsistencies in the use of terminology for 'black' across various surveys, opinion polls and research data, the fragmentation of the various communities that encompass the 'black' group is a consistent feature. There are also differences within specific communities; for example the proportion of Afro-Caribbean women with academic qualifications is the same as for white women, while Afro Caribbean men have fewer qualifications than their white counterparts. According to certain social and economic indicators, Indians are on a par with, if not performing better than, whites – for example, on performance in secondary schooling and in the number that go on to higher education. Indians certainly perform better than Afro-Caribbeans on most economic and social indicators. Yet statistics reveal great disparity within the various Asian communities. The most alarming is the poor showing of Pakistanis and Bangladeshis, 60 per cent of whom are manual workers and 68 per cent of whom have no educational qualifications.[9]

Moreover, the impact of such diverse economic and educational levels across and within ethnic groups has a negative effect on political resources. While interest is one factor in being involved in mainstream politics, having the skills, experience and fortitude needed to participate effectively is still another matter. Black people generally do not have the same organisational and financial resources available to them as whites.

This lack of readily accessible resources has often made black organisations beholden to the mainstream for their financial viability and organisational credibility. Inevitably the allocation of limited grant-aid funds has fostered further divisions and inter-group rivalry. The main source for such funding is at local authority level. And the distribution of such funding of voluntary groups by local councils is a prime example of 'too few funds chasing too many organisations'. The result is that decisions are not based just on need. Less tangible and unidentifiable factors influence the decisions, thus making the allocation even less meritocratic and objective. Such is the nature of things in the voluntary sector. Some encouragement is to be found in the growth of black voluntary organisations; their dependence on governmental funding, however, makes them 'quasi-governmental' agencies on the local level. This relationship in some respects defines and predetermines the nature and scope of their involvement in the community – rendering them less autonomous than at first glance. The value of the black voluntary sector, however, cannot be underestimated in terms of providing black people with much needed organisational and leadership skills – resources that are essential for black political empowerment.

This leads us to the fourth important factor affecting black political participation: the location of the black population. Because black people are disproportionately located in urban areas the impact of their involvement tends to be localised. The high density characteristic of the black population has drawbacks in terms of building a national base but is fertile breeding ground for local political involvement. Similarly, the dense political geography affects the availability of political resources making them also more accessible on a local level. Even within given cities, black people tend to occupy certain areas, providing them with 'pockets of power' but making it harder to obtain large spheres of influence.

The reality is that black people can wield tremendous political clout in certain wards, for example the University ward in Bradford whose 90 per cent turnout rate has repeatedly elected an Asian councillor.[10] Yet ward monopoly is not necessarily enough to support a black parliamentary candidate (that is to say one who might run independently of the major political parties).

The political experience of black people within the mainstream, even on a local level, is often clouded by individual if not institutional racism. Racism is the most recurrent and pernicious factor affecting black participation in the political arena. Its effects are well documented in the political experiences of many of the activists interviewed in this book. Their testimony stands as an indication of the extent to which racism affects those who chose to be active and is also the source of fear on which many black people's 'inactivism' is based.

Despite these obstacles, black people have nurtured a rich tradition of political activism. Mainstream party politics remains an option, and is discussed in the succeeding chapters of this book, but for many black activists grassroots activity continues to hold the most attraction and offer most rewards.

Community Activism

Black self-organisation has been the main source of preservation for black people in Britain and is a vital component of their future political progress. While conventional political power is vested in mainstream political institutions, more immediate success for blacks has traditionally come by placing their political energies into grassroots activism. Black community organisations vary greatly in their size, resources, ability to mobolise and the degree to which they are 'representative' of the community at large. Likewise, many of the community organisations which directly influence black life are not solely comprised of black membership: many are dependent on community alliances that cut across racial lines and have often included coalitions with white liberals. Some of the most successful initiatives have occurred through the collaboration between black activists and Labour's left. The now defunct GLC, with its extensive programme of resourcing black groups, promoting anti-racist activities, and organising events to celebrate cultural diversity, stands as a good example of successful past efforts.

Throughout the early years of large-scale migration, black organisations were often connected with the politics of their native country, while their participation in Britain centred on the British labour movement. These newly arrived black migrants were completely excluded from the political mainstream and lacked the resources to affect seriously state action. The position of the black community during the 1940s and 1950s resulted largely in the 'tacit acceptance' approach to race relations (see chapter 1), which linked in to the governments' stance of 'non interference'. However, despite political exclusion and disenfranchisement, black people still managed to develop their own political organisations, albeit on a local level and of a limited scope. The active black immigrants never forgot their commitments back home nor did they fail to realise the need for forming political alliances in this country. Joining forces with white workers in the labour movement seemed the most natural progression. Such organisations as the Caribbean Labour Congress and the Indians Workers' Association grew out of and flourished from the concerns of life in their native country and from the dissatisfaction of life in England.

The Caribbean Labour Congress (CLC) was founded in 1945 as a political organisation for West Indian trade unionists. It had its origins in the Caribbean but some of its migrant workers established a London branch. The chief purpose of the CLC was to promote national liberation and to stimulate economic and political growth in the West Indies. Most of its activities, therefore, were focused on raising funds and providing material support for their comrades back home. With the advent of the Cold War, the CLC's Communist affiliation made it the target of government harassment. The CLC still received, however, the respect of substantial parts of the labour movement. It takes the credit for publishing the first postwar black political journal in Britain called the *Caribbean News* which was the forerunner to the *West Indian Gazette*. The *Caribbean News* provided detailed accounts of black support for liberation movements around the world and told of black workers' solidarity with white workers in disputes such as the dockers' strike of 1954, while also mounting poignant attacks against the 'colour bar' and overt racial practices especially in the work place. Trevor Carter was an active member of the CLC and best describes the precarious position of black workers:

> The daily grind most of us faced was the reality of racism wherever we
> looked ... alongside our battles against the employer, black people have
> always had to fight to gain recognition of their existence in and
> contribution to the labour movement ... We found it difficult in the
> fifties to understand white workers' lack of sympathy towards our
> particular problem as immigrants ... Wages and conditions were one
> thing but the politics of colonialism was quite another.[11]

The tragedy was that white workers did not support their black
comrades with the same intensity nor with the same sense of
obligation. How quickly solidarity was forgotten, for the white
dockers in 1968 were among those who demonstrated in support of
Enoch Powell's infamous 'rivers of blood' speech. Nevertheless
black political thought in the main retained its commitment to a
left politics which tended to be 'blind' to race, and which located
the main struggle as being one in which all workers, regardless of
race, battled against capitalism and imperialism. In spite of the
white labour movement's failure to prioritise issues of importance
to black people, commitment to the labour movement was still seen
as the only means of economic and social liberation.

The Indian Workers' Association (IWA) Great Britain[12] began in
the 1930s. Like the CLC, it was formed with the twin goals of
promoting economic and political change in India and with the
hopes of becoming a part of the British trade union and labour
movement. Initially, autonomous IWAs were formed in cities with
large settlements of subcontinental Asians. After 1947 when
independence was won for India and Pakistan, the IWAs
concentrated more on domestic affairs and the problems of
migrants in securing citizenship, decent jobs and housing. The
various IWAs become centralised under one general national body
in 1958 with branch status given to local associations. In 1967 there
was a big split within the IWA, which had never been a unitary
grouping. It left two groups: the more militant group known by
their leader, IWA (GB) Avtar Jouhal and the Indian Marxist
sympathisers, the IWA (GB) Prem Singh.[13]

Despite the divergence, the IWAs were united on the common
objective of combating all forms of racial discrimination. As
anti-racist and anti-fascist campaigning organisations, the IWAs
often combined with other black groups in joint efforts such as the

Campaign Against Racist Laws (CARL) and the Campaign Against Racial Discrimination (CARD), and they were founding members of the Black People's Alliance formed in 1968 as response to the growing racist sentiments legitimised by Powellism.[14]

Once again the prevailing view was that racism was the tool of capitalist oppression, and therefore, the struggle against racial supremacy was inseparable from the creation of a strong and united working-class movement. Their support for the trade union movement, however, did not blind the IWA to the racism that was promulgated by the movement. Nor was the Labour Party seen as the natural haven for the IWA's electoral support. On the contrary, the IWA often challenged the policies and leadership of the Labour Party. In particular, there was much criticism of the Wilson government for issuing a White Paper endorsing and strengthening the 1962 Commonwealth Immigration Act. Similarly, the IWA has been very suspicious of the state-controlled race industry, seeing the Commission for Racial Equality (CRE) and all of its predecessors as the state's attempt to 'white-wash' black politics. As such, the IWA urged its membership not to be a part of the smoke-screen and actively campaigned against what it regarded as some of the organisation's more objectionable policies. While the IWA supported Labour, as being, of the two main parties, the one which is more in sympathy with its objectives, some of its members have openly spoken out against the Black Sections Campaign, viewing it as separatist and not an appropriate way to bring about racial harmony.

The West Indian Standing Conference (WISC) is another long-standing black organisation which, like the IWA and the CLC, has had a substantial impact on black British politics. It differed, however, in that it was not so solidly linked to the labour movement. WISC was the beginning of a new breed of black organisation that recognised the need for a tactical change in approach. These new organisations that began to develop in the 1960s served increasingly a brokering function on behalf of the black community to secure the provision of much needed services.[15]

Founded in the aftermath of the 1958 Notting Hill riots, WISC continues to serve as an umbrella organisation for a network of West Indian affiliated local groups and societies. Its lobbying efforts on behalf of black people in the field of education, mental health, welfare rights and policing has made it a strong political force in the black community. The myriad of organisations under its auspices and the divergence of its scope gave WISC during its heyday a considerable mobilising strength. The key to its success was its ability to attract a diverse membership of West Indians and black people of non-island origins, specifically Africans. The reality of their shared plight against a common oppressor and the necessity of mutual co-operation, caused black people to subsume their individual island identities into the common recognition of West Indian. The diversity of membership in WISC reflected this recognition of the need for unity and ranged from associations of black sporting and social clubs to employment-related groups of health professionals and teachers, as well as encompassing the spectrum of political opinions from conservative to radical.[16]

WISC was pre-dated and largely influenced by the League of Colored People which was effectively the British version of the American NAACP (National Association for the Advancement of Colored People). The League was founded by Dr Harold Moody in 1931 and was mostly a fund-raising vehicle, dependent on the financial generosity of white liberals. It served chiefly a social function, providing numerous cultural and civic events in the black community. WISC, by contrast, was more of a political organisation, actively engaged in the struggle to eliminate racial discrimination and promote equal opportunity for all. WISC, which celebrated its thirtieth anniversary in 1988, continues to publish a journal called *Team Work* and currently boasts some 31 affiliated groups as members.

The 1960s was the decade of a critical 'awakening' for black political self-organisation. Not only had the myth of 'returning back home' begun to dissipate, the succession of events of this decade transformed the nature and focus of black self-organisation. Stringent immigration control was the order of the day and no political party when in office was exempt from trying its hand at it. The 1962 Commonwealth Immigrants Act was the work of Macmillan's Conservative government but the next Labour government under Wilson further tightened the reins by issuing the White Paper in 1965 entitled, *Immigrants From the Commonwealth* and by passing the 1968 Commonwealth Immigrants Act.

Black political organisation during this critical period of the 1960s developed along two strands. First, there was a proliferation of black organisations that operated on the politics of resistance and protest, and that defined the black British plight squarely in line with the struggles of peoples of colour all around the world. Their origin and membership was deeply planted within the community, although their views were not completely representative of all segments of the community. These resistance organisations were prototypical of later grassroots activism. Such organisations included the Black Panther Party and the Black Unity and Freedom Party (BUFP), both of which grew out of the United Coloured Peoples' Alliance (UCPA). These groups were founded on the slogans of 'Black Power' ushered in so visibly by the now famous clenched fist salute of the black American medalists at the 1968 Mexico Olympics which broadcast to the world that it was okay to be Black and Proud.

The contributions of these groups have largely gone unnoticed in modern commentary. Although they were often small and disjointed with a relatively short lifespan, their major contribution was in providing a new mode of political expression for a disenfranchised, alienated and frustrated black population. Theirs was the recalcitrant voice of resistance to mainstream political oppression, and the force of cultural pride and black nationalism. It was these early black protest groups which created the political space for ethnic minorities to define their own 'blackness': 'During those days, there was a mutual recognition amongst black people as we passed each other on the street – "Hello, my black brother" ', recalls one former Black Power activist. 'It was a matter of pride, simple decency and respect for one another.'[17]

The Black Power movement created a mood and style, providing a platform for black activism which nurtured a pool of black community activists who have continued to be a source of black leadership. Out of these types of organisations came such publications as *Race Today*, and the *Black Liberator*, and such individuals as Darcus Howe, Frank Crichlow, Michael de Freitas (alias Michael X) and poet Linton Kwesi Johnson. Political commentators and historians from left and right have dealt these groups a fatal blow, often describing them as fringe fanatics that have been counterproductive to the establishment of racial equality in Britain. Attempts by the media and press were made at every turn to discredit these protest organisations. They were portrayed as a threat to law and order and systematic efforts were made to weed out such 'undesirables'. However their influence has been important in developing black self-organisations.

The Mangrove: A Model of Community Activism

One of the symbols of resistance during this era was the Mangrove Community Association. The Mangrove was a bulwark of community activism: in its thirty-one year history, the Mangrove served as a centre for black culture and political expression and as such it was the object of countless attacks by the police.

The Mangrove began its life as a restaurant by that name in North Kensington in 1969. Its owner was a Trinidadian, Frank Crichlow, who emigrated to England at the age of twenty as an accomplished musician. He envisioned the place to be a local 'hang-out', where black people could congregate to stay in touch with their roots – the sights, sounds and smells of the Caribbean. The Mangrove restaurant was an extension of an earlier establishment, the Rio Coffee Bar, also owned by Crichlow in the late 1950s. The instant popularity of these establishments was an illustration of the extent to which the black immigrant population was searching for its cultural identity. Crichlow best explains the special need that the Mangrove filled for the black community in these early days:

> The Rio was the starting point, out of it came the Mangrove. The beautiful thing about the Mangrove was the way it brought West Indians from all over the Caribbean together. The island differences were put aside. We were all in the same boat and we were looking for friends. The Mangrove became a meeting place. Black people from all over London and England would come, meet, eat, exchange ideas, learn ... It blossomed from there. Without any plans for getting into community politics, I found myself in a position as owner of the place as a leader – people would look to me for advice and if they got into trouble they would call on me.[18]

The crowds that the Mangrove drew soon began to attract the attention and suspicion of the police. The Mangrove became the focus of police harassment with one unwarranted raid after another.

After three drug raids during the summer of 1970, none of which found any drugs or resulted in any arrests, the black community in Kensington staged a march to express their solidarity and to send a clear signal to the police that they were not going to be intimidated by their scare tactics. The 9 August demonstration, assembling more than three hundred protesters, began at the Mangrove and proceeded to the two police stations in the area. Confrontation with the police resulted in the arrest of some twenty-six protesters and attracted tremendous publicity. What had started as a peaceful local protest had exploded into a national outburst on the state of race relations in Britain and was followed with a personal witchhunt by the state to find somewhere else to place the blame. 'We were shocked that the protest had made the headlines', Crichlow recalled. 'C.L.R. James had warned us that the fact that we made the front pages was a sign that they would be after us. He was spot on!'[19]

The Home Secretary Reginald Maudling called for an inquiry into the disturbance which resulted in the arrest on charges of rioting, assault, affray and conspiracy of what became known as the 'Mangrove Nine': Frank Crichlow, Darcus Howe, Barbara Reese, Althea Lecointe, Rupert Boyce, George Millet, Rhodan Gordon, Antony Innes, and Roddy Kentish. The 1971 trial lasted for 10 weeks during which daily demonstrations took place outside the Old Bailey to protest the injustice of their prosecution. It was a tremendous display of black unity and an important early example of black self-organisation. 'My source of strength came from the black community. On the day the decision came down to look out in the courtroom at a sea of black faces was inspiring', Crichlow remembered. In the end, the Mangrove Nine were vindicated and the police evidence was shown to be both conflicting and fabricated. They were acquitted of the rioting charges and received suspended sentences for other minor offences.

During the mid-1970s, the Mangrove was turned into the Mangrove Community Association and continued to serve the black community. It provided an array of different welfare and advice services for helping with accommodation, legal and employment problems. It organised numerous events and activities to get black youths off the streets, like the Mangrove steel band. The Mangrove also continued its political role in exposing police harassment and mobilising protest against racial discrimination in Britain and abroad. In 1988, it registered as a charitable foundation, the Mangrove Trust, which helped to ease the financial strain that a growing constituency had caused over the years. The Trust took over the voluntary work of the Mangrove Community Association and allowed the Association to remain a separate entity to pursue its political and campaigning efforts. In March 1988, the Mangrove Trust entered into a partnership with the Abbeyfield Trust to provide housing to black pensioners. The Abbeyfield/Mangrove became a registered housing association and the Mangrove was given half a million pounds by the Housing Corporation and the local authority to develop the project. July 1990 was the official opening of the facility for the elderly which provides accommodation for six black pensioners.

The housing project represents a successful collaboration between the grassroots and the mainstream in an effort that will directly benefit the black community. Jebb Johnson, the director of the Mangrove Trust, acknowledged the irony: 'Here was a relationship developing between the old establishment, the Abbeyfield which has the Prince of Wales as its patron, and a radical black organisation. There were fears on both sides but the principle of providing shelter housing to the elderly was paramount. It was a common denominator.'[20] As a housing association, the Mangrove Trust can place bids on properties and have an important voice in the planning and development of its neighbourhood. There are plans to develop additional Abbeyfields and for an ex-offenders' hostel to deal with black criminal rehabiliation.

Despite the success of the Mangrove's community involvement, the police harassment still persisted. The raid on 24 May 1989 was potentially the most damaging attack. This time Crichlow was planted with heroin during the confusion and was charged with possession and drug trafficking. During the trial which followed, the police's own technology worked against them. The reading on the camera used by the photographer at the time of the raid revealed the inconsistency of the policemen's testimony, allowing ample time for the heroin to placed on Crichlow. Crichlow was again acquitted but not after suffering substantial financial and emotional anguish due to the injunction that banned him from the Mangrove for the year leading up to the trial. Crichlow's personal trials have been compounded by the recent closure of the Mangrove with large debts. Despite its demise, however, the Mangrove has served as a source of inspiration for an entire generation of community activists.

The emergence of a black counterculture in the 1970s created the conditions for more mainstream participation. As Crichlow noted: 'We are the necessary link that keeps those mainstream activists grounded and binds them to the community at large.' Throughout the recent history of black people in Britain, protest has served as the catalyst which placed racial equality on the public agenda. This is a parallel process to that in the USA, where the inconceivability of compromising with Malcolm X made negotiating with Martin Luther King more appealing. The establishment is forced, if you like, to chose between the 'lesser of two evils'.

This brings us to the second strand of black self-organisation that grew out of the awakening of the 1960s – the brokering/ campaigning groups which served more as a liaison with the establishment. Instead of being located necessarily within the black community, these groups were self-professed 'representatives' of black concerns. They were generally more broad-based than the protest groups, and were conciliatory in nature, calling for political integration rather than separatism. Their demands were less polemical, characterised by universalist appeals to human decency – like the right to equal opportunity, elimination of racial discrimination and promotion of racial equality. Their membership attracted a different type of activist, usually middle-class black and white liberal professionals.

Lobbying the Mainstream: The Rise and Fall of CARD

The Campaign Against Racial Discrimination (CARD) was the first widely recognised national campaigning organisation for ethnic minority interests in Britain. It began in late 1964 as a pressure group and was aimed at defending an 'interest against discrimination and to promote the cause of general social reconstruction and social equality in Britain'.[21] In pursuing this goal, CARD sought to perform two functions: first, a lobbying function, to influence national and local public policy regarding discriminatory legislation; and second, a mobilising function in organising and unifying disparate black groups to create a social and political movement. Benjamin Heineman in his book, *The Politics of the Powerless*, provides the most in-depth study of CARD and suggests that it was the incompatibility of these two functions which eventually lead to its failure. The organisation was doomed from its inception because CARD was founded to speak for a social and political movement that did not exist, while simultaneously trying to create the movement with neither the power nor resources to make it work.[22] Nevertheless, the failure of CARD provides an important perspective for future attempts at developing national black organisations and is an interesting case study in the conflicts that often arise in anti-racist campaigning.

From its genesis, CARD had as one of its objectives the creation a national black civil rights movement in Britain that would mirror in structure and purpose the American movement going on at the time. In fact, the inspiration for the organisation came from Dr Martin Luther King who, while in London *en route* to Stockholm to receive the Nobel Peace Prize, held a private meeting with some 30 Commonwealth immigrants and a few white sympathisers.[23] King's visit to Britain was timely: racial tensions were high and there was deep concern amongst blacks and whites that race relations were worsening. Only months before King's arrival in December 1964, Patrick Gordon-Walker, a Labour frontbencher, was defeated by a blatantly racist electoral campaign in Smethwick. Concern over this overt incitement to racial bigotry dovetailed with debates on the forthcoming Race Relations Bill of 1965, and to an extent made it easier to swell support for any solution that sought to halt the devastating effects of inter-communal conflict.

King was the external stimulus, but the primary leadership initiative came from Marion Glean, a West Indian Quaker activist who was the founder of 'Multi-Racial Britain', a forerunner of CARD. It was Mrs Glean who organised the private meeting with King and who hand-picked the people who would attend. She drew initially from the pool of black immigrant activists and white liberal sympathisers who had worked with her on Multi-Racial Britain, namely C.L.R. James (West Indian writer and critic), Ranjana Ash (member of the Movement for Colonial Freedom), Theodore Rosak (then editor of *Peace News*), Michael Randle (close associate of *Peace News*) and his contact, Bayard Rustin (the American civil rights leader who planned King's itinerary in London and arranged the meeting with Glean), and Barry Reckford (West Indian playwright and actor). Mrs Glean also invited members from the leading anti-racist organisations like WISC, IWA-Southall, the West Indian Student Union, Anti-Apartheid, the British Caribbean Associations and the Council of African Organisations.

King encouraged the group to place pressure on the government by organising opposition to any discriminatory legislation. There followed a second meeting on 20 December at Marion Glean's house attended by eighteen people who became the nucleus of CARD. The group was officially formed and named CARD on 10 January 1965. 33 people attended the inaugural meeting, a third of whom represented immigrant groups, almost all London-based, and a sixth of those present were white. The Executive Committee were elected. A seasoned Labour Party activist and Grenadan doctor, David (now Lord) Pitt, who had stood as a Labour candidate in Hampstead during the election of 1959, was elected chairman of CARD. With one exception, the rest of the members elected for the Executive Committee were not active members of any existing immigrant organisation nor could any of them claim to belong to the working class, black or white. Aside from Pitt, the other seven members of the Executive included Glean herself, Richard Small (law student and aide to C.L.R. James and founder of the West Indian Student Union), Gurmukh Singh (member of the Committee of 100), Selma James, Anthony Lester (a white barrister and member of the Society of Labour Lawyers), Dr Ranjana Ash and Autar Dhesi (member of the Southall IWA).

There was much acrimony early on over the extent to which CARD should align itself with the existing mainstream political institutions, especially with the Labour Party given its decision to extend the Commonwealth Immigrants Act of 1962 through its subsequent 1965 White Paper.

The ideological rift between Pitt and Glean epitomised the divisions within CARD that would continue throughout the group's existence. Glean argued for a separate political existence for CARD without close association with Labour or the trade unions, while Pitt was more chiefly concerned with co-ordinating an effective anti-discrimination lobby for the organisation and therefore acknowledged the need for alliances with the more sympathetic elements of British society. The split as characterised by Heineman was between the working majority led by Pitt and the dissidents led by Glean. There are many ways to describe the division. In a superficial sense, it was a schism between the 'realists' who thought that legislation was the paramount and critical first stage of the process, and the 'romantics' who 'were going to raise up the coloured masses with a clarion call'.[24] Ideologically, it was a split between the centre left and the radical left.

As chairman, it was Pitt's leadership which largely determined the direction of the group. His preoccupation with the legislative function of the organisation meant that the group's resources were used mainly on drafting and lobbying for anti-discrimination laws. 'The reason why legislation loomed so large', Pitt revealed, 'was because we felt very strongly that you could not really get any basic changes unless you get laws changed. While you may help change attitudes via campaigning, you needed the backbone of the law in order to be really effective.'[25] The dissidents who wanted a mass social movement were left alienated and frustrated. Many were angry about the white liberal presence in the organisation and accused the leadership of being 'hijacked' by its white supporters. Pitt argued that there was never any doubt who should control the focus of the group, the problems arose when the work had to be done:

> When we were laying down the basics for CARD, we said that it should be controlled and based on the experiences of the victims of discrimination and the others, the whites, as supporters. In practice, however, our supporters were very active. Often more than we were.[26]

Thus the seed of contention had been planted.

The development of CARD was heavily influenced by the black American experience. They looked to the American exemplar when drafting equal opportunity legislation. The US Civil Rights Act of 1964 became the model for demands by CARD on the implementation of anti-discrimination provisions and served as an example for the 'lobbying' wing of CARD. Among the dissidents, there were constant references to the need to replicate the activities of such black American organisations as the Congress for Racial Equality (CORE), the Student Non-Violent Co-ordinating Committee (SNCC), the National Urban League and the NAACP.

The mass movement supporters of CARD argued that Britain should also use the direct action approach of picketing, economic boycott, sit-ins, and concentrate on developing strong communities of immigrants. But ironically this attempt to replicate the American civil rights movement was to be another source of CARD's demise. The experience of blacks in the USA had a distorting effect on the movement in Britain since it assumed that race relations in Britain would undergo analogous stages, yet such an assumption did not pay sufficient attention to the specifics of the British situation.[27]

Despite internal division, CARD still managed to make a significant yet limited contribution to race relations legislation. During its first six months, CARD's involvement included parliamentary lobbying for amendments to the Race Relations Act of 1965. The Act only dealt with discrimination in public places and CARD's aim was to put into place 'proper conciliation machinery' so that institutional racism in housing and employment could later be addressed. CARD mobilised a successful lobbying operation to educate MPs, through letters and personal briefing, and sought to heighten public awareness through the press. Its proposals on anti-discriminatory laws in housing and employment served for two years as the basis for discussion and eventually was adopted in the Race Relations Act of 1968, much to the chagrin of the TUC whose objection prevented the provision from being included in the first Act of 1965. But even CARD's impact on this front was limited since, during the critical period in 1967-8 for lobbying on the proposal's passage, CARD was in a state of immobility and protracted confusion – detached from the political establishment and disowned by the community it sought to represent.

The CARD's small measure of success was chiefly as a pressure or promotional group. Its capacity to affect change was significantly impaired, as Heineman aptly observed:

> As a promotional group, CARD depended on the goodwill of others. It could make no threats, exercise no sanctions. It could not claim the right to be consulted, it could not negotiate or bargain. It could not force people to act. The source of its 'power' was its ideas and information and it could only persuade and hope that the lessons were sympathetically received.[28]

The demise of CARD was laden with omens for future

developments. The organisation was riven with internal antago-
nisms stemming from personal differences in approach, leadership
styles and ideological beliefs. The organisation's sense of
powerlessness revealed itself through factions. It was inevitable
that a coalition of people from divergent backgrounds, experiences
and political orientations, would produce mounting frustration
ultimately leading to paralysis. The tension finally came to a head
during the group's annual conference in 1968. The radical faction
moved resolutions that changed the structure of CARD and in the
process alienated and offended the white liberal elements. Aside
from the internal divisions, there was the recurring conflict
between CARD and pre-existing black organisations, like the West
Indian Standing Conference (WISC), over the role that each should
play.[29] This type of infighting overshadowed even the moderate
success achieved by CARD.

The irony was that CARD was unable to do even with its own
organisation what it sought to do throughout British society as a
whole. It aimed to create a movement that would encompass all
races, all classes, cut across generational and educational variants,
and embrace all religious and ideological differences by appealing
to universal concepts of social equality. But such ecumenical
phrases as 'justice for all', 'equal opportunity' and 'social cohesion'
were empty platitudes which were not enough to sustain its own
unity, let alone a mass social and political movement in Britain. To
this extent, CARD was a victim of its own rhetoric, its own inflated
ambition. Despite its manifest failings, Pitt defends CARD's record
unabashed:

> I never regarded what happened as too much of a tragedy, for the pure
> and simple reason that having got the legislation, we established the
> 'machinery' for acting against discrimination. All the machinery that has
> been established (Race Relations Board, Community Relations
> Councils and the Commission for Racial Equality), we helped to
> implement.[30]

Tragically, this very 'machinery', which stands as CARD's major
contribution, has been most bitterly criticised: the CRE
celebrated the 25th anniversary of the first Race Relations Act to
clamouring charges of its incompetence and failure to change
positively the quality of race relations in Britain.[31] One is

immediately reminded of the oft-quoted statement of A. Sivanandan, the director of the Institute of Race Relations, that 'the Commission took up the black cause and killed it'.[32] Pitt argues, however, that the Commission was not allowed to succeed, blaming both the low status and priority it was given by the Thatcher government and the insistence of the establishment on always selecting a white person to head the Commission.

> The machinery does reflect a prejudice. The official attitude has always been that they (whites) need to be working *for* us not *with* us. They need to be the leaders, perhaps because they don't believe we can do it.[33]

With the development of the 'race relations industry', has the brokering role of black organisations which developed during the 1960s become irrelevant? Goulbourne suggests another adverse interpretation of the CRE and similar 'conciliatory machinery' which he terms 'parastatals':

> Both the Community Relations Councils and the Commission for Racial Equality exist to co-ordinate the state's efforts in establishing a modicum of peaceful co-existence between groups perceived to be caught up in a conflict between different elements in civil society. These parastatals have themselves, not unexpectedly, assumed much of the functions of the broker ... absorb[ing] potential leaders of community-based broker groups.[34]

It is unlikely that the function of black community activism will ever become extinct. As long as the vast majority of black people are cut off from mainstream participation, grassroots organisations must continue to thrive.

The success, therefore, of black organisations cannot be judged solely on mainstream standards of effectiveness – most specifically, the ability to manipulate public policy decisions. Although they have largely failed to exercise direct influence on the formulation of policy, black organisations have exerted tremendous pressure indirectly by raising important grievances and demanding immediate redress. Similarly, while attempts at building a broad-based national black organisation have met only with mixed success, single-issue campaigns have been more successful in this regard.

The effectiveness of single-issue campaigns lies in the ability to focus and galvanise large-scale support towards a finite, specified objective over a relatively short period of time. It is not surprising then that one of the immediate responses to the failure of CARD was the formation of a single-issue organisation, the Joint Council for the Welfare of Immigrants (JCWI), which was successful in carving out a particular niche by fighting immigration and nationality issues while remaining relatively apolitical. Other single-issue campaigns have sprung up around specific incidences of police harassment, as with the Mangrove Nine and cases of criminal injustice like the Bradford Twelve. One of the most memorable and effective single-issue campaigns, which elicited the support of white people as well as black, arose as a response to the increasing use made by police of the 1824 Vagrancy Act which empowered them to conduct unwarranted harassment of black youths. The 'Scrap SUS' campaign not only resulted in the repeal of the law, but was also regarded as an important example of the force of alliance-building in a national campaign.

Self-organisation has continued to be a vital part of black community activism, generally taking three forms based on need-specific, policy-specific and individual-centred campaigns. Need-specific organisations fulfill the needs of a certain group of blacks that share common experiences, in welfare or employment. Black professional societies like the Society of Black Lawyers, of Black Doctors and so on, which emerged with some success in the 1980s. Even the Black Sections movement could be classified as a need-specific organisation since it addresses the particular needs of black Labour Party members. Policy-specific organisation are those that are established to attack certain policy decisions locally, nationally and/or internationally. Examples include the Anti-Apartheid Movement, Campaign Against Racist Education (CARE), and immigration organisations like the Southall Monitoring Group. The third current form of black self-organisation is individual-centred campaigns which are usually appeals and petitions against injustice for specific individuals on issues such as deportation and doubtful conviction. One of the more high-profile examples was the campaign for the Broadwater Farm Three who were found guilty of murdering PC Blakelock during the 1985 riots on the Tottenham estate. This campaign eventually resulted in the quashing of the convictions of the three.

Despite the failure of past efforts, the most recent attempt to form a mass, umbrella organisation has been made by the National Black Caucus (NBC). Its effort is worthy of some attention, if only to point out where it seeks to overcome the problems that defeated CARD.

The National Black Caucus: Developing a National Movement

The National Black Caucus grew out of the disillusionment of black delegates who participated in the 1986 annual conference of the National Council of Voluntary Organisations (NCVO) on 'Changing the City' in Manchester. They were shocked at the lack of inclusion of the black experience in a conference with a topic so clearly related to this issue. Concerned about the non-participation of black people in urban policy, the black conference delegates formed the National Black Caucus and issued a demand to the NCVO that it provide the resources for a separate conference for the black voluntary sector on the inner cities. The three-day residential conference entitled, 'Black People Pushing Back the Boundaries', was held in Nottingham in April 1987 and attracted more than 200 participants from across the country. During that conference a 'planning group' was chosen with the task of organising a second conference and of establishing a network of individuals interested in discussing and developing strategies for change.

The NBC presently functions as a national umbrella organisation for affiliated black groups and individuals. Its main role is to collate and disseminate information of relevance to the black communities, and to devise strategies for the co-ordination and implementation of all policies and issues pertinent to the lives of black people. Unlike CARD with its close affiliation to the Labour Party, the Caucus purports to be an 'apolitical' organisation willing to do 'business' with whichever party is prepared to address the needs of the black community. It is divided into some eight regions throughout the country and is governed by the Planning Group which meets in different areas every four to six weeks. It is further divided into sub-groups that control certain policy concerns like Housing, Economic Development, Health, Education, the Arts and Social Services.

It is the belief of the NBC that 'only by building an independent black movement outside traditional white party structures can black people effectively bring about change on our terms.'[35] The NBC and the Labour Party Black Sections movement often attract the same supporters. But the NBC differs in that they regard Black Sections' association with the Labour Party as confining the political development of black people. The fact that NBC is ostensibly grassroots and that it is formally apolitical reflects a major improvement on CARD. However, like Black Sections, its ability to develop a mass unitary black movement in Britain will be severely impeded by the internal divisions within the black community, and by unsympathetic public perceptions. The challenge for NBC, of course, is to develop a movement despite these obvious obstacles and the history of similar attempts that have run into the sand.

The tremendous appeal of grassroots activism is that it necessitates self-reliance. It means black people defining and addressing their own agenda in a manner they have determined to be most appropriate for them. Increasingly, however, the success of black self-determination has required collaborative efforts with the mainstream – the political establishment, the media and business. The character of contemporary political participation has been one of growing *interdependence*. The effectiveness of the separate, external structure of black self-organisation of earlier decades is almost unimaginable today. With the advent of a brokering role for many black organisations in the 1960s, contact with the mainstream, especially to attract funding, became inevitable and this has changed the nature and scope of community activism enormously.

'Grassroots', as a descriptive term for community activism, has become a misnomer for many organisations – considering the reliance on mainstream financial support for so many black voluntary organisations. This calls into question whether any community organisation can truly represent its people and deliver the service goods to its constituency without some assistance and co-operation with established institutions, albeit informally. The Mangrove Community Association provides a case in point. Its recent joint effort with the Abbeyfield Trust to build sheltered housing for black pensioners would never have been possible in the 1950s and 60s. But this dependency works both ways. The mainstream has become equally reliant on the talents and leadership of the black activists who often work within the 'race relation industry' serving, ostensibly at least, as points of liaison with their black communities. Jebb Johnson of the Mangrove Trust is extremely cynical: 'They either buy us off, jail us or kill us off. Those blacks with positions in the race industry are a part of the first strategy. They give these guys positions and they will push paper and not be very effective.'[36]

The increasing number of black activists brought into positions of power – however limited – within local authorities, in race units, housing and social services, might at one time have been seen as a policy of 'appeasement'. But now a dual approach – of working within and outside mainstream politics – is the key to black political empowerment. The danger, of course, lies in the prospect of those black activists working within the establishment losing sight of their responsibility to the community they represent. The outcome is, therefore, dependent on the ability of black people in the main-stream to keep their 'eyes on the prize'. Realism, however, dictates an acknowledgement of the fact that black activists are needed within the system because one cannot keep knocking at the door unless someone is inside willing to open it.

Notes

1. Stuart Hall, 'The Gulf Between Labour and Blacks', *The Guardian*, 15 July 1985, p. 18.
2. Marian FitzGerald, *op cit*, pp. 104-5.
3. Greater London Council, 'Survey of Political Activity and Attitudes to Race Relations' (Second Report), 1985, p. 7.
4. Michael J. Le Lohé, 'Voter Discrimination Against Asian and Black Candidates in the 1983 General Election', *New Community*, Vol. 11, Autumn/Winter 1983, pp. 101-8.
5. Zig Layton-Henry and Donley T. Studlar, 'The Electoral Participation of Blacks and Asians: Integration or Alienation?' *Parliamentary Affairs*, Summer 1985, pp. 312-3.
6. Colin Brown, *Black and White Britain: The Third PSI Survey*, Policy Studies Institute, London 1984, pp. 19-20.
7. *Ibid*, p. 157.
8. Kenneth Newton, *Second City Politics: Democratic Processes and Decision-making in Birmingham*, Oxford University Press, Oxford 1976, p. 231. Cited in FitzGerald, *Black People and Party Politics in Britain*, Runnymede Trust, London 1984, p. 20.

9. Labour Force Survey Data, 1985-7.

10. Muhammad Anwar, *Race and Politics*, Tavistock, London 1986, p. 58.

11. Trevor Carter, *Shattering Illusions: West Indians in British Politics*, Lawrence & Wishart, London 1986, p. 52. See also pp. 45-55 for more detailed account of the CLC.

12. Indian Workers' Association (GB) is distinct from IWA Southall which was formed in 1956 and is not officially affiliated to the IWA (GB). IWA Southall is chiefly a campaigning group in Southall and does not have the broad-based support that the IWA (GB) enjoy.

13. More in-depth research on the IWA can be obtained from: Sasha Josephides, 'Principles, Strategies and Anti-racist Campaigns: The Case for the Indian Workers' Association', in Harry Goulbourne (ed.), *Black Politics in Britain*, Avery, Aldershot 1990, pp. 115-30. Additional sources are John De Witt, *Indian Workers' Association in Britain*, Oxford University Press, Oxford 1969, and Rashmi Desai, *Indian Immigrants in Britain*, Oxford University Press, Oxford 1963.

14. Josephides, *op. cit.*, p. 119.

15. Harry Goulbourne, 'The Contribution of West Indian Groups to British Politics', *op. cit.*, p. 101.

16. *Ibid.*, p. 103.

17. Interview with Frank Crichlow, 13 June 1990.

18. *Ibid.*

19. *Ibid.*

20. Interview with Jebb Johnson, 14 June 1990.

21. Benjamin Heineman Jr, *The Politics of the Powerless: A Study of the Campaign Against Racial Discrimination*, Oxford University Press, Oxford 1972, p. 3.

22. *Ibid.*, p. 1.

23. *Ibid.*, p. 34.

24. *Ibid.*

25. Interview with Lord Pitt of Hampstead, 22 June 1990.

26. *Ibid.*

27. Heineman, *op. cit.*, p. xi.

28. *Ibid.*, p. 121.

29. *Ibid.*, chapter 5.

30. Interview with Lord Pitt, *op. cit.*

31. *The Guardian*, 'Acts but no Real Faith', 13 June 1990.

32. Cited in FitzGerald, *op. cit.*, p. 60.

33. Interview with Lord Pitt, *op. cit.*

34. Goulbourne, *op. cit.*, p. 104.

35. The National Black Caucus Conference materials, 'Networking the Black Community', 1988.

36. Interview with Jebb Johnson, *op. cit.*

3 The Tories and Liberal Democrats

Which side do they cheer for? Are you still harking back to where you came from or where you are? I think we've got a real problem in that regard. If you say to a lot of people out there in the street Tebbit is a racist, they'll scratch the back of their heads and say, Well so am I. If that's what being a racist is, then I'm one as well.

– Norman Tebbit

Although the Labour Party has the highest level of black involvement (see chapter 4), the efforts of the other political parties have posed a credible threat to Labour's ethnic minority stronghold in recent years. In their different ways, both the Conservative and Liberal Democrat parties have tested the loyalty of Labour's black vote, and have facilitated a limited degree of black political participation within their own structures. Given that it has been the party of government for over a decade, it seems logical to look first at the changes in the Tory Party.

The Conservative Party

The history of the Conservative Party's approach to black people and racial issues has been plagued by illiberalism. More than any other party, the Conservatives have been known as the party 'toughest' on race. This perception of the party stems partly from the legacy of widely publicised antics of such Tory populists as Peter Griffiths, who in 1964 at Smethwick ran perhaps the most famous bigoted campaign in British history; Enoch Powell, MP for Wolverhampton South West, whose immortal words still 'foam' like his own metaphor, the 'River Tiber'; and Harvey Proctor, former MP for Billericay, who as recently as 1987 launched a vigorous campaign to repatriate 'coloured immigrants'. Conservative institutions such as the Monday Club and the right-wing intellectual thinktank grouped around the *Salisbury Review*, have served to provide a respectable intellectual gloss for such policies. The Conservative Party leadership has in general tended to distance itself from these inappropriate actions, attempting to repudiate the inference that these incidents were very possibly indicative of the views of the majority of Tories. But it has on many occasions made use of populist measures to win support from right wing 'anti-immigrant' forces.

While it is true that such extreme views represent only a vociferous minority in the party, the most damaging and inexcusable statements are those made by high-profile Tory government and party officials. Remarks such as those of the former Conservative Party chairman, Norman Tebbit (quoted above) are quite alarming. The crude insensitivity of Tebbit's comments is graphically illustrated by his suggestion that the preference between cricket teams is somehow an indication of one's 'Britishness'. The insinuation is obvious: ethnic minorities must forego all their historical and cultural links in order to be truly British – or rather 'English'. This appeal to an exclusive category of 'Englishness', the ideology of the 'island race', is a recurring theme in Conservative Party statements on the issue of race.

Perhaps the most notable controversial comment of recent years was made by then Prime Minister Mrs Thatcher on 30 January 1978 when, in a Granada Television interview, she publicly committed her administration to a populist anti-immigration viewpoint, stating 'if you want good race relations, you have got to allay people's fears on numbers'.[1] She asserted that people were afraid that Britain and its character would be 'swamped' by people with different cultures. Mrs Thatcher went on to observe that neglecting the issue of immigration had driven some people to support the National Front and that she hoped to attract to the Conservative Party those voters who had been supporting the National Front: 'we are not in politics to ignore people's worries but to deal with them'. The impact of these words was astounding. Within days of the interview, it was reported that Mrs Thatcher received some 10,000 letters, many from Labour voters and most of whom supported her views.[2]

Election polls even suggest that it was with the influence of these remarks that the Conservative Party comfortably captured the Ilford North seat from Labour in the March by-election held that year. There is little doubt that Mrs Thatcher's notorious 'swamping' speech set the tone for her first administration's fierce assault on immigration, promptly leading to the passage of the 1981 Nationality Act. Such a position illustrated perfectly Mrs Thatcher's view of Britain as essentially white and Anglo-Saxon. A fear of difference and diversity, unconsciously or otherwise, underpinned the 'one of us' attitude that Thatcherism embodied.

There is of course a non-Thatcherite, more liberal, strand in the Tory party, represented by Ted Heath. His administration had a considerably better record on issues of race. Although it was the Heath government which introduced the 1971 Immigration Act, he expressly forbade Tory candidates from exploiting the immigration issue during elections. He had also shown his inclination to eliminate such abuse when he removed Enoch Powell from the Shadow Cabinet in 1968 after his 'rivers of blood' speech. In contrast to the cultivated intolerance of the new right intellectuals, Heath went on record stating, 'there is no reason why cultural diversity should not be combined with loyalty to this country'.[3] Moreover, Heath honoured Britain's commitment to the entry of Ugandan Asians in 1972, in contrast to Labour under Callaghan which reneged on a similar pledge to help the Kenyan Asians in 1968, and instead passed the Commonwealth Immigrants Act to keep them out.

This 'liberal' strand within the Tory party is still in existence, and it seems that John Major, at least on the question of individual discrimination, has some allegiance to this tendency. However the Conservative Party still continues to draw considerable support from the 'anti-immigration' constituency, and has been accused of 'playing the racist card' on the issue of the Asylum bill.

Thatcher and Race Relations

Mrs Thatcher first came to power in 1979, coinciding with a period in which race became an important electoral issue. The bi-partisan consensus to keep race out on the 'periphery' was beginning to break down as pressure for firmer immigration control mounted – opening a proverbial can of worms. The Thatcher government was ushered in with the promise of reform of citizenship and nationality laws, and much of the first year of her administration was occupied with the passage of such legislation. The riots of 1980 and 1981 further ensured that racial issues would play a prominent role in her first term. In both the passage of the 1981 British Nationality Act and her handling of the riots, Thatcher fashioned her own style of economic liberalism mixed with political and social authoritarianism. This involved a combination of self-reliance and personal responsibility with a strong emphasis on law and order. Thatcherism was an eclectic panoply of free market economics, a strong state, Victorian morality, and an obsession with national sovereignty and military preparedness. The paradox of her administrations was that her policies required 'rolling back the state in some instances [but being] fiercely interventionist in other ways'.[4]

Pioneering strategies to 'roll back the state', Mrs Thatcher privatised several public utilities, cut income tax rates, especially for higher earners, removed exchange controls, abandoned price and income policies, and encouraged the deregulation of minimum wages. All these measures fostered a new type of economic individualism which has had adverse implications for the collectivist ethic of the welfare state. Like 'Reaganomics' in the USA, Thatcherism during the 1980s in Britain reinforced Ivan Boesky's slogan that 'greed is good', which works well enough for those in society who start with the resources to seize the opportunities. The problem with Thatcherism, like Reaganomics, was that little or no safety net was provided for those who do not start with such advantages. In theory, the whole society should benefit from greater prosperity and economic efficiency, but in reality a form of social Darwinism takes over and only the 'fittest' in society are able to survive. The 'unacceptable face of Thatcherism' was that the burden of blame for this distributive problem was placed on the victims of poverty, not on the system which impoverished them.

Thatcherism translated into race relations exercised a mixture of firm control over immigration policy and tough policing, with noninterference in private forms of discrimination in employment, education and housing. In the private sector, the Tory government allowed legislative measures such as the Race Relation Acts to suffice without giving teeth to their enforcement. James Goodsman, former Head of Community and Legal Affairs at the Conservative Central

Office, acknowledges the party's refusal to take the lead in fighting racial discrimination:

> The philosophy of this government is a non-interventionist one: that government doesn't interfere with the way people run their businesses, providing they don't contravene legislation. It is not part of the way that this government sees that it should go.[5]

Consistent with this philosophy, the Tories passed up the opportunity to initiate an effective and co-ordinated national policy on race relations following the crisis of the riots in 1980 and 1981. The government's reaction to the riots in Bristol (1980) and Brixton (1981) was to shift any responsibility for the incident away from them. The official government notices, and much of the press and media coverage, chose to couch statements in terms of black youths' 'lawlessness'. Headline after headline sensationalised the events by reinforcing received images of mobs of unruly black people running riot through the streets. The 'racialisation' of the riots centred on the theme of law and order, while little attention was focused on the underlying conditions that caused it. Roy Hattersley's suggestion that poverty, unemployment and deprivation were the causes of the disturbance met with much ridicule on the parliamentary floor from Enoch Powell who took this opportunity to elucidate his intemperate views:

> Are we seriously saying that so long as there is poverty, unemployment and deprivation our cities will be torn to pieces, that the police in them will be the objects of attack and that we shall destroy our own environment? Of course not. Everyone knows that, although those conditions do exist, there is a factor, the factor which the people concerned perfectly well know, understand and apprehend, and that unless it can be dealt with – unless the fateful inevitability, the inexorable doubling and trebling of that element of a population can be avoided – their worst fears will be fulfilled.[6]

Indeed, it was the use of terminology like 'that element of a population' which allowed Powell and other neo-conservatives again to link social problems to the immigration issue.

When the Scarman Report came out in November 1981, the causes of the riots were characterised both in terms of oppressive policing and deprived conditions which, he noted, created a 'predisposition towards violent protest.' Lord Scarman called for direct action by the government to alleviate the factors which led to this 'predisposition'. His recommendation to implement economic and social policies to alleviate the social problems which contributed to such situations was not welcome to the Tory government. As John Solomos notes in *Race and Racism in Contemporary Britain*:

> Scarman's call for more direct action to deal with these problems, along with racial disadvantage, posed a challenge to the political legitimacy of the policies which the Government had followed from 1979 onwards. Having spent the whole summer denying any link between its policies and the riots, the Government had to tread warily in responding to the economic and social policy proposals.[7]

The government was much more willing to respond to the suggestions regarding the role of the police and to advise on restoring law and order than to heed any demands for national action against discrimination in housing and employment, although Michael Heseltine, then at the Department of the Environment, put forward a limited series of inner city initiatives, such as the setting up of Enterprise Zones and the institution of the International Garden Festival in Liverpool. This failure to take decisive action on the questions of racial discrimination and equality of opportunity helped to harden the perception of Conservatives as 'tough' on race and represents further proof to black Britons of their illiberalism.

Black Participation and the Conservative Party's Response

Nevertheless, no Party could afford to ignore black people as voters completely. Conservative initiatives for recruiting black support began in earnest as early as the mid-1970s. After two successive defeats in 1974, party leaders showed a greater willingness to explore alternative sources of votes. The special CRC report on the October 1974 election concluded that ethnic minority voters were crucial in determining the outcome in numerous marginal constituencies. The report revealed that thirteen of the seventeen seats gained by Labour in October 1974 were in constituencies where the majority was less than the black population. The implications to the Conservative Party were clear: failure to appeal to black voters had contributed to their electoral defeats. The CRC findings were further endorsed by the 1971 Census estimates that the black population was increasing in numbers to become a distinctive part of the electorate, especially in urban areas. In fact, the Census revealed that black people comprised 8 per cent of the population in at least 61 constituencies. These indices were enough evidence for Conservative Party officials to initiate efforts to alert their members of the growing importance of the ethnic vote.

Ironically, despite the Party's negative image among black Britons, it was the Conservatives who first established formal mechanisms for incorporating black supporters within the party. In January 1976, the Central Office Department of Community Affairs was formed and the new department was given the task of promoting better relations between the Party and certain target groups within the community – skilled workers, ethnic minorities and young voters. A special Ethnic Minorities Unit was also established within the Community Affairs Department to spearhead efforts specifically aimed at improving the Party's image within the black community. It was through this unit that the Anglo-Asian and the Anglo-West Indian Conservative Societies were first formed. These two Conservative Societies were created as a means of recruiting ethnic minorities into the Party. Members of the societies were Tory sympathisers, black and white, who wished to promote ethnic minority participation within the Party. Membership of the Conservative Party was not a prerequisite for joining the societies; the idea was to have a visible presence in the ethnic minority communities, which was sponsored by the Central Office and offered representations on the local and national committees of the National Union of Conservatives.

The Anglo-Asian Conservative Society was the larger and more successful of the two societies. Organised by Narindar Saroop, a Conservative councillor in Kensington and Chelsea and the Society's first chairman, the Anglo-Asian Conservative Society was the primary focus of the ethnic minority recruitment effort. Greater emphasis was placed on appealing to Asian voters since they were perceived as 'naturally conservative'. At its peak, the Anglo-Asian Conservative Society had approximately 30 branches around Britain and its national membership was ostensibly half Asian and half white. The society exerted, however, only minimal influence on policy decisions within the Conservative Party: its activities centred mostly on social functions rather than on political debate.[8]

The Anglo-West Indian Conservative Society was also established in 1976 under the leadership of Basil Lewis, a West Indian Conservative Councillor for the London Borough of Haringey. Unlike its Asian counterpart, the Anglo-West Indian Conservative Society was solely London-based and was less prolific with only ten branches at its height.

This activity was nevertheless tempered by the over-riding fear of alienating the white skilled workers whom the Party was also courting with growing success. Even though some efforts were made by Party officials to appeal to black voters, it was still clear that the rank and file Tory members in the local constituencies did not share the same sentiments. The Conservative Party steadfastly maintained its hostile stance on immigration control. At Party conferences, resolutions regularly appeared demanding repatriation of ethnic minorities. The message was clear: the 'race card' would continue to be played when it most benefitted the party.

No one appeared more willing to play the race card than the then Party leader, Margaret Thatcher. With Mrs Thatcher at the helm, overt efforts to appeal to black voters would always be viewed as an electoral liability. Further proof of her resolve was found in her veto of the Party's participation in the Joint Committee Against Racialism (JCAR), a group formed in the autumn of 1977 charged with the task of promoting racial harmony and composed of members of all the political parties, the British Council of Churches, the National Union of Students, the British Youth Services, the Board of Deputies of British Jews and leading immigrant organisations. Mrs Thatcher thwarted Tory efforts to appoint John Moore, MP, as joint chairman of the JCR along with Labour's nominee Joan Lestor, MP, because she disapproved of the Party's involvement in an anti-racist movement that she regarded as dominated by left-wing groups. She was adamant about the Party's dissociation even though participation by the Party had gained overwhelming support from the Executive Committee of the National Union of Conservatives. Indeed, this was the nature of the Thatcher legacy on race – a blend of limited and pragmatic commitment to woo a section of black voters, combined with outright and ideologically based antagonism to any rhetoric of anti-racism.

By the 1980s, the Anglo-Asian and the Anglo-West Indian

Conservative Societies had lost much of their credibility. There had always been scepticism as to the role of the two Societies within the Party and it had been questioned whether they fostered fuller participation as opposed to a further marginalisation for minorities. By 1986 the Societies had been dissolved amid political controversy. Growing divisions within the Anglo-Asian Society surfaced when it became controlled by Sikh supporters of an independent Khalistan. The Society's new-found proclamations threatened serious damage to the Conservatives' intergovernmental relations with India and upon the recommendation of the National Union they were disbanded.

Soon after, an alternative – the One Nation Forum – was formed as a multi-racial organisation functioning as an advisory body to the National Union. It was envisaged as a more tightly controlled body than its predecessors and, as its name suggests, was intended to signal the unitary and uniformly 'British' society the Conservative Party sought to promote. Unlike the Societies, membership of the One Nation Forum is organised on a selective basis by invitation of the Party chairman, undoubtedly providing more effective control by the Party leadership. Presently, there are approximately 60 members of the Forum, including representatives from all the main ethnic minority communities and from the Party leadership. It is divided geographically into three constituency liaison committees: the North, Midlands and the South, which includes the most active London Liaison Committee. The objectives of the One Nation Forum as listed in its brochure are:

(1) to discuss all matters relating to ethnic communities and, where thought necessary, to submit findings to the Party Chairman and Ministers concerned; (2) to respond to requests for information and reactions from Ministers and the Party Chairman; (3) to encourage the growth of ethnic minority membership in constituency parties and increase ethnic minority participation and activity in constituency associations; and (4) to spread Conservative principles and philosophy through the ethnic communities.

The Forum has all the trappings of being a more influential body, headed up by an impressive list of Tory Party officials. The first chair of the Forum was Peter Morrison, then Minister for Energy and for a brief period Lord Young also served. For the first time provisions for minority representation at Party level were guaranteed with two seats on the Executive Committee of the Conservative Party reserved for the Forum. Despite the hype, however, the One Nation Forum in its five-year existence has actually done little more than its precedessor. Most of its political activities coincide with social functions serving chiefly as useful networking opportunities for ambitious black Tories. Several of the black candidates who stood for the party in 1987, however, point to the great potential of the One Nation Forum as an avenue for recruiting more black people into the party. John Taylor, former political advisor at the Home Office and twice parliamentary candidate (whose selection and subsequent defeat in Cheltenham became something of a cause célèbre), asserted:

> The One Nation Forum is an acknowledgement of the Conservative Party's commitment to truly building Britain into a more unified multi-racial nation. It's not like a black section, in the sense that we seek to incorporate the ideas and sentiments of all parts of this nation to really reflect within the Forum the multi-racialness of the society. We want to be a pressure group from within and bring together any perceived divisions. The Forum, I feel, will greatly aid the advancement of blacks in the Conservative Party in the future.[9]

While black voters, as a group, still remain among Labour's most loyal supporters, these initiatives have resulted in some progress being made towards recruiting black Conservative members. The Party's approach to recruiting ethnic minorities has been typical of the Conservative style of politics generally. The emphasis is on the creation of a meritocratic society in which people are allowed to succeed to the best of their ability. This approach to race relations is based on the notion that Britain is being transformed into a society that judges people, not by the colour of their skin, but on their ability to do the job best.

By constructing an image of itself as the 'colour-blind' Party, the Conservatives have sought to appeal to black voters. This approach to the recruitment of ethnic minorities is actively promoted by the Conservative Central Office, as the then Community Relations Officer, James Goodsman was keen to demonstrate:

> We are always on the lookout for support from all parts of the community. We try not to differentiate between them. We don't use colour, or racial or ethnic background as a method of differentiating

between people. And we try to appeal to the population as a whole not to have black sections and that sort of thing.[10]

This 'colour-blind' approach was first given a national profile during the campaign for the 1983 general election. The Party placed an advertisement in the press which showed a young black man dressed in a business suit above the caption 'Labour says he's black. Tories say he's British'. The advertisement went on to espouse the now familiar Tory rhetoric, launching a scathing attack on Labour's approach to race relations:

> With the Conservatives, there are no 'blacks', no 'whites', just people.
> Conservatives believe that treating minorities as equals encourages the majority to treat them as equals.
> Yet the Labour Party aims to treat you as a 'special case', as a group all on your own.
> The question is, should we really divide the British people instead of uniting them.

This campaign propaganda created much acrimony, especially among the black press, causing many publications to refuse to publish it. Several black groups issued public statements condemning it as insulting and degrading to black communities, while the right-wing press seized the opportunity to exploit the issue provoked by the advertiser's copy.

Even with their contentious efforts to appeal to black voters, the Tories continued to be plagued by the openly racist elements of the Party. No less than seven resolutions appeared in the Immigration and Race Relations section during the 1983 Party conference and this was a decline from the 34 'tough on immigrants' resolutions in 1981. All but one of the 1983 resolutions made inflammatory demands calling for an end to all immigration, repeal of the Race Relations Acts and repatriation of immigrants.[11] Once again the persistence of populist hardline conservatism on race overshadowed more liberal Tory initiatives and damaged efforts to appeal to the majority of black people.

Black Tories

Until recently, the existence of black Tories represented a flat contradiction of the traditional image that the Conservative Party conveyed. Black Conservatives are generally perceived as an enigma – misunderstood and often taunted by their own community. They appear to be suspended between two worlds – a black community unwilling to accept their political affiliation and a party tarnished by a history of racial intolerance. Why then do black people join the Conservative Party? What is the appeal, and what is the extent of their support?

The archetype of the black Conservative Party member tends to differ greatly from that of the black Labour Party member. It is largely assumed that the black Tory is atypical of the black population as a whole both in socio-economic terms and in an unwillingness to identify with their ethnic minority background.[12] Black Conservatives tend to have above-average educational and occupational qualifications and to place less emphasis on ethnic identity. Many black Tories are impressed by the Party's 'colour-blind' approach to ethnicity, viewing it as an indication of the Party's commitment to equality. Joyce Sampson, co-ordinator of the London Liaison Committee for the One Nation Forum, joined the Conservative Party for just that reason:

> Because it is a party that doesn't think in terms of black and white, it is the right one for black people. What is done in the Conservative Party is done for everyone, you are not going to get on in the Conservative Party because you are black – you will get on whatever you do based on your merits. It is a meritocracy. I don't want to be given something just because I am black. I want to work for the things I achieve like anyone else and achieve them because I do it better.[13]

The Conservative Party is quite aware of the type of black activist it is most likely to attract. Recruitment efforts are usually targeted at Afro-Caribbean and Asian businessmen and women, and those sections of the black community which have traditionally valued principles of self-help, and moral and civic responsibility, with which the Party is most closely associated. 'Black people vote Conservative because they are usually Conservative-minded', explained Lurline Champagnie, a long-time Tory supporter and Party member who was the Conservative parliamentary candidate for Islington North in the 1992 General Election. 'They want their children to succeed. They don't want someone saying to them, "Oh you are a poor old thing." We are hardworking, independent people. We want to get up and go.'[14]

This view of the Conservative Party as the party of self-improvement and choice strikes a similar chord with another prominent black Tory, Nirj Deva, a successful Asian businessman, 1987 Conservative parliamentary candidate for Hammersmith (and subsequently elected as MP for Brentford and Isleworth in 1992):

> The Conservative Party believes in a self-help society. I don't want to be patronised and told that I am feeble and require the help of other people like the Labour Party does. Fortunately, the Tory Party never does that. We take away the patronising image.[15]

For many British Asians voting Conservative is the most obvious choice, concluded Deva:

> Asians are naturally conservatives, with a capital and a little 'c'. They believe in profits, in enterprise, home-ownership, religious education, children and families – all of it is Conservative and all the things that the Party is talking about.

Asians are not the only minority group for whom the Conservative values are held to appeal. West Indians have also been attracted to the party for similar reasons. John Taylor explained why he joined the Conservative Party:

> I took a look at all the manifestos of all the main political parties. It was the Conservative Party's traditional values which stood out for me ... It [the Tory manifesto] was talking about the traditional values like strong family units, discipline in the schools, discipline in the homes. Those things appeal to me ... The Conservative party was the party which was actually saying something. I have no regrets.[16]

As support generally for the Conservative Party reached its peak in the 1980s, so too was there a marked increase in black membership and representation in the party. The numbers of black councillors increased as did the number of black prospective parliamentary candidates. In the 1979 general election, there were twelve black candidates standing but only five were representatives of the three main parties. Two Conservative candidates were among them: Farooq Saleem for Glasgow Central and Narindar Saroop, former leader of the Anglo-Asian Society, who stood in Greenwich. Their candidacies represented the first time the Conservative Party had selected ethnic minority candidates to fight in a general election since 1945.[17] The number of black Tory parliamentary prospectives rose to four by the 1983 general election, while the total number of ethnic minority candidates increased to eighteen. But once again the black candidates all fought in unwinnable seats. In 1987, a total of 27 black people stood for election and six were black Conservatives. Although details of their election results are analysed elsewhere (see chapter 6), it suffices to say here that none had a chance of winning and only one actually resulted in a (0.4 per cent) swing towards the Tory Party – John Taylor who fought Birmingham Perry Barr. The Conservatives' increase in black parliamentary candidates from two in 1979 to six in 1987 was greatly overshadowed by the rise in black Labour candidates from one in 1979 to fourteen in 1987 which included the triumphant election of the first black Labour MPs.

While the commitment to black representation appears to have relaxed presently, the Tories have witnessed two high profile appointments. In 1990, a black Tory became the first black woman in the House of Lords when Shreela Flather, former Mayor of Windsor and Maidenhead, was made a Baroness and thus at that time the only black Tory sitting in either House of Parliament. In the same year, John Taylor had the distinction of being the highest ranking black civil servant when he was chosen as a special advisor to the Home Secretary, then David Waddington.

There were eight prospective black candidates chosen to fight at the 1992 General Election: Lurline Champagnie, for Islington North, challenging a 9657 Labour majority; Abdul Zayyum Chaudhary, in Birmingham Small Heath, facing a 15,521 Labour majority; Nirj Deva, who was candidate in Brentford and Isleworth, following the retirement of sitting MP Sir Barney Hayhoe, who held a majority of 7,953; Mohammed Khamisa, in Birmingham Sparkbrook, facing Roy Hattersley's 11,859 majority; Andrew Popat in Bradford South, where Labour MP Bob Cryer had only a 309 majority; Mohammed Riaz in Bradford North, against a 9514 Labour majority; Mohammed Rizvi in Edinburgh Leith, against an 11,327 Labour majority; and John Taylor, contesting the Conservative held seat in Cheltenham. Of these eight, clearly the most promising prospects were for Nirj Deva, John Taylor and Andrew Popat. The other five candidates had virtually no chance of success. However it is promising that the Conservative Party in the 1992 election increased the number of black candidates, and also the number of black candidates with a real chance of election.

Officials at Conservative Central Office are encouraged by the growing numbers of black Tories. This growth is due in part to the increasing size of the black middle class which flourished during the economic boom of the 1980s. The burgeoning number of black professional and social societies are regarded by Conservatives as a natural pool from which to draw. But just as the economic climate has changed in the 1990s with a marked recession, so too could this fertile seed-bed of black recruits dry up. John Taylor, however, does not view the future with pessimism, but as a transitional period:

> It's a natural reaction to the 1980s. It's time for a quieter revolution for blacks in Britain; a time for blacks to concern themselves with creature comforts – to become bankers, homeowners and educators ... It's the Conservative Party who will benefit from this process.[18]

Estimates suggest that there are twenty to thirty Afro-Caribbean and Asian members on the Central Office list from which Tory parliamentary candidates are chosen. Goodsman pointed to the decrease in racist resolutions presented at conference and the increasing number of black faces at Party gatherings, as evidence of the Party's changing attitude towards black political participation. He acknowledged, however, that the real problem lies in getting Conservative constituencies to select black candidates:

> Where there is still a problem is in getting ordinary Party members to say 'Yes, we want a black person to represent us in the House of Commons'. Now it will come. It is one of those inevitable things. I mean you can't get a tide to go back when it's coming in.[19]

Perhaps this statement was somewhat optimistic in the light of subsequent events in Cheltenham, however.

Race After Thatcher: Major's 'Classless Society'

As John Major stood in front of Number 10 giving his first speech as Prime Minister, he spoke of making Britain a 'classless' and open society where every person can make it on their merit. If this was mere Conservative rhetoric, it at least sounded more genuine given Major's background. But his vision of the 'classless society' faces formidable obstacles augmented by the trying conditions of recession and increased unemployment which heighten the divisions between the haves and have-nots within society. His wish for equality of opportunity for all, regardless of origin, has already been sullied by racist incidents in the embarrassing public row over John Taylor's candidature in Cheltenham.

Regardless of the patience and perseverance of black Tories and the intentions of some party officials, the rank and file Tory members are still unprepared to see, let alone embrace, black representation within the party. It is this unacceptable face of Toryism which has returned to haunt the Party's efforts to recruit, retain and promote black leadership.

On the eve of the Tories' election of Major as the youngest Prime Minister this century, history was also being made in the Conservative constituency of Cheltenham. John Taylor was chosen to fight the seat left vacant by the retirement of Sir Charles Irving, MP who served for 16 years. Taylor was one of four candidates chosen for interview from more than 250 competitors including such political mavericks as former MP Peter Bruinvel beaten by Keith Vaz in the 1987 election. Taylor was adopted by the constituency's selection committee by a majority and he was subsequently the only candidate on the shortlist brought before the general body for approval. He narrowly secured the nomination by a vote of 111 to 83.

His selection was immediately met with overtly racist comments from several Conservative constituency members. Most notorious were those made by Bill Galbraith who was quoted in the press as saying that Cheltenham should not 'give in to a bloody nigger even though Central Office have foisted him upon us'. A self-employed publisher, Galbraith went on to embellish his comments in subsequent interviews:

I don't think we want a bloody nigger to represent us in Parliament. What I said was what many people think. Would you vote for a black man to represent the town of Cheltenham? There are plenty of niggers in London but would you vote for a black man in the country town of Cheltenham?[20]

Other local Tory members were equally upset with Taylor's candidacy but were much more subtle in their response. Their opposition was in coded form: they opposed his selection because they wanted a 'local man' to represent them in Parliament. Undoubtedly a 'local man' would be white in this country town with a black population of less than 1 per cent. Steadfast and determined, Taylor remained committed to fighting the 'Persil white' seat. 'I have a job to do', he professed. 'It is a very enjoyable job and it is getting to know the people of Cheltenham.'[21] The Conservative Central Office strongly backed Taylor's selection. In response to the controversy surrounding Galbraith's remarks, John Major made a statement in the House of Commons that 'as long as I am privileged to lead this party, it will never become an exclusive club.'[22] In a written reply to Roy Hattersley he stated:

> I will have no truck with racism ... My hope is to build a truly open society in which every man and woman should be able to go as far as their talent, ambition and effort take them. There should be no artificial barrier of background, race or religion.[23]

However, the controversy generated by Taylor's candidacy calls into question the Conservative policy of ignoring issues of race.

The very image the Conservatives have long cultivated of colour-blind meritocracy was seriously compromised. Taylor was in every sense an excellent choice – a trained barrister, Conservative councillor in Solihull, parliamentary candidate in 1987 and former adviser to four ministers at the Home Office. If merit was the only consideration, surely there would not have been a controversy. Yet his candidacy tested not only current Conservative ideology but also the old political belief that people vote for parties not individuals. Has the ghost of David Pitt's 1964 defeat in the once-safe Labour seat of Clapham been resurrected? Until the illiberal attitudes of the rank and file Tory supporters and members change, irrespective of the Central Office's initiatives, the Tory Party's effort to recruit black support, as history suggests, will encounter great difficulties.

The Liberal Democrats: 'Clean but Untested'

Pragmatism rules. The Alliance failed to attract the black vote because black people, as do all people, vote for a party they think is going to win. So long as it looked as if the Party was going to win, it got support. But as long as the Party has no prospects of getting into power than it won't get votes regardless of its record on race.[24]

These words from Roy Evans, a former member of the Social Democratic Party (SDP) National Executive Committee, typifies the dilemma that crippled the Liberal/SDP alliance and continues to hurt its progeny, the Liberal Democrats. The dilemma has become a vicious circle – unless the party can win it cannot recruit more supporters, but without increased support it cannot possibly win. The awkward irony is that the former Alliance parties – the Liberals and SDP – which were predecessors to the Liberal Democrats had perhaps the best record on race of any of the major parties. But without mass support and proportional representation that record will remain just symbolic and untested. This section traces the political origins of the Liberal Democrat Party and the historical commitment to fair immigration policies and racial equality of the two parties that combined to form it.

The Liberal Party

Historically, the Liberals have proven to be stalwart fighters against racial discrimination and for the rights of immigrants. At times when the other two parties sought to restrict the flow of immigrants, the Liberals opposed such measures and held fast to the tenets of nineteenth-century liberalism that the free movement of people across national boundaries was necessary in order to promote cultural, intellectual and economic exchange. Thus the Liberals have opposed all of the major immigration provisions introduced by both Labour and Conservative governments since 1962. It was the only party to reject the 1968 Commonwealth Immigrants Act, while Labour and the Conservative Parties formed a bi-partisan alliance in favour. The Liberals also led the opposition in protesting against the 1971 Immigration Act, as well as the 1981 Nationality Bill, and the government's recent limitation on the issue of passports to the citizens of Hong Kong.

In repudiation of the 1981 Nationality Act and the subsequent riots, the Liberal Party published a report commissioned by its leader David Steel called *Inner City Disturbances* in which the party denounced the efforts to halt immigration as 'deplorable', adding that the measures were 'designed to keep out coloured immigrants rather than to control immigration generally'. As early as this the Liberals were also espousing ethnic monitoring, condemning the Tory government for removing the ethnic question from the census and thereby removing 'the possibility of monitoring the effectiveness of government policies designed to ensure equality of opportunity'.[25]

It should be noted, however, that local Liberal parties do not have quite such an untarnished record. In 1986 the Liberals took control of the London Borough of Tower Hamlets amid criticisms that they had pandered to the racist vote. They initially abandoned ethnic monitoring, in spite of the party's national stance, and proceeded to evict many homeless Bangladeshi families. This, at the very least, cast doubts on the party's 'clean' image on racial issues.

Liberals were themselves early campaigners for the principle of equal opportunity and formed the founding members of the Joint Committee Against Racialism (JCAR) in 1977. The anti-racist sentiments ran deeper than official party rhetoric: surveys revealed that Liberal voters also viewed racial equality as important. One poll by the British Election Study of 1984 revealed that 42 per cent of Liberal voters believed that attempts to ensure equality for black people in Britain had not gone far enough compared with 23 per cent of the Tory supporters.[26] In the 1979 election manifesto, the Liberals pledged to protect and defend the rights of minorities and called for a 'comprehensive law outlawing discrimination on the grounds of race, sex or political beliefs with enforcement through a single Anti-Discrimination Board'.

The Liberal Party sought to address the concerns of ethnic minorities through the Community Relations Panel, which was chaired until the mid-1980s by Lord Avebury, widely respected as a champion for racial equality. The Panel was established to aid the Party in its recruitment of black members and to advise the party on issues of race and immigration. Lord Avebury spearheaded several campaigns to encourage minority support for the Party including personally writing in 1980 to all the local chairs urging them to adopt black candidates and to encourage black membership drives in their community. As part of a national recruitment effort, the Liberal Party in 1982 launched a special campaign actively seeking out black support. During the campaign, the Liberals sent out policy statements and position papers to black organisations and held a press briefing for the ethnic minority press at the House of Commons to announce their new initiative.

Electorally, however, their policy and campaigning efforts did not yield the desired results. Liberal strongholds are not geographically located in areas of high ethnic minority concentration. While there are a few black Liberal loyalists, researchers have found that the Party is more apt to win 'personal votes' depending on the candidate running and the constituency.[27] The Pakistani support for the Liberal MP, Cyril Smith in Rochdale has often been cited as an example of the personal appeal of Liberal candidates. Because of Cyril Smith's personal contact and links with the ethnic minority community, he was able to win his first election in 1972 by a majority of 5,000 on the strength of the Rochdale Asian voters who switched their support from Labour to Liberal reportedly in numbers as large as 6,000.[28]

Despite the Party's inability to attract national black support, it has consistently selected black candidates to run in parliamentary elections. Since the election of Dabodhai Naoroji as a Liberal MP in 1892, even when the two other major parties were reluctant, the Liberals have consistently fielded at least two black candidates. The Liberals' efforts to attract black voters was to a great extent aided by its alliance with SDP. Together, the Parties' black support rose from 5 per cent of the black vote in 1979 (for the Liberals) to 11 per cent in 1983 for the Alliance.[29] However the desertion from Labour to the Alliance was proportionally much smaller than the swing in the white working class.

The Social Democratic Party

When the SDP burst onto the British political scene in 1980 promising to break the mould of the two-party politics, its early promise attracted many newcomers – first-time Party members. Disillusioned by what they perceived to be the patronising attitude of the Labour Party and alarmed by the hostility of many Conservatives, some black people were among the political novices who came to the SDP. From the outset, the Party was ideologically and intellectually attractive, threatening to take support away from both sides of the political spectrum. It was more conciliatory than

Labour towards the European Community, while less aggressive than the Tories on social issues of housing and education. But its occupation of the middle ground, which initially won it support, would ultimately lead to its demise, for the Party could not continue to be 'all things to all people'.

The SDP's anti-racist stance was clearly articulated in its constitution: 'The Social Democratic Party exists to create an open, classless and more equal society which rejects prejudices based upon sex, race or religion.' Two of the most prominent Party leaders had proven credentials on race. Roy Jenkins, now Lord Jenkins of Hillhead, was the first leader of the SDP and, as Labour Home Secretary under Callaghan, he drafted much of the race relations legislation. Similarly, Shirley Williams, the first SDP President, had earned a reputation as a proponent of racial equality as one of the instigators of the Labour Party Race Action Group. She was also instrumental in setting up the SDP's direct action campaign on race. The Social Democratic Campaign for Racial Justice (SDCRJ) was organised as a multi-racial body that operated mainly within the party as an interest group to influence the party on issues that affected ethnic minorities. The Campaign for Racial Justice was the closest thing the Party had to a formal mechanism for recruiting black people. 'It was not a success', commented Roy Evans, once a leading SDP activist. 'Its strength and ability to fulfill its objectives depended on the strength of the Party and so, as the Party decreased, so the influence of the campaign diminished, because no one would listen to the Party'.[30]

Black activists, however, did exert influence within the party. Two black people won elections on to the SDP national executive committee in open competition with other members of the party. Dr Lutfe Kanal and Roy Evans were chosen from a list of candidates including numerous high profile personalities. Roy Evans credits his win to the Party's use of proportional representation and suggests that it's the SDP's espousal of proportional representation which should have attracted more black support:

I was chosen before Anthony Sampson because, although I did not receive many first preference votes but enough to keep me going, by the time the votes of the others had been transferred I was getting all the seventh and eighth choice votes. It illustrates why proportional representation is a way in for black people.[31]

Although the SDP had ethnic minority candidates fighting both local and parliamentary elections, like its Liberal partners, it still had problems winning mass black support. Regardless of its anti-racist position, the fact that it appeared unelectable did hinder its efforts. Both Parties came quickly to the conclusion that there was not enough room for four political parties in British politics, that only by combining their efforts could either Party stand a chance.

From the Alliance to the Liberal Democrats

For the 1983 and 1987 elections, the two Parties fought as the Alliance. The manifesto for the Alliance parties in 1983 called for sweeping measures to eradicate racial discrimination and inequality, while embracing the principle of positive action to achieve equal opportunity. Reaching a compromise, the Alliance promised to amend the 1981 Nationality Act instead of the total abolition to which the Liberals had been committed. The 1983 manifesto outlined the Parties' concern to reinstate the right of British citizenship to all children born in Britain and in addition, to provide measures to limit the official discretion exercised in granting citizenship by instituting a right of appeal process. With regard to immigration, the Alliance went on record as saying it would be in favour only if the controls were used in non-discriminatory ways and only in a manner that did not seek to break up the family unit. Moreover, the Alliance promised to introduce a UK Bill of Rights and to create a Commission of Human Rights which would incorporate the Commission for Racial Equality and the Equal Opportunities Commission. Most significantly, it underlined its commitment to proportional representation.

The Alliance parties had an excellent showing in the 1983 election winning 25 per cent of the popular vote, but because their support was so evenly spread out across the nation, the first-past-the-post system ensured that this would only translate into 23 seats, whereas Labour's 27.6 per cent of the vote gave them 209 seats. In that election, the Alliance got an estimated 11 per cent of the black vote, while the CRE exit survey revealed the Conservatives got 7 per cent with Labour once again as the biggest winner.

In the 1987 election (see chapter 6), the Alliance's performance was a disappointment. It secured 23 per cent of the overall vote to Labour's 32 per cent and the Conservatives' 43 per cent. A Harris survey on voting intentions revealed that 7 per cent of the Afro-Caribbeans and 10 per cent of the Asians intended to vote Alliance. The emerging reality was that black electors look to more than a Party's record on race when deciding whom to vote for.

The eventual collapse of the Alliance and the subsequent formation of the Liberal Democrats left the Party battle-worn. David Owen's brief split with the remaining SDP loyalists, while the majority formed the Liberal Democrats, was doomed to failure and further loss of credibility for its leader. The Liberal Democrats remain true to their forbears' record on race, but it remains to been seen whether this commitment will ever be given the opportunity to stand the test of government.

As for attracting the black electorate, the Liberal Democrats welcome black support when they receive it, but – like the Tories – do not expect mass defection from Labour. The prospects of attracting black support for the Liberal Democrats look as negligible as they were for the Alliance parties. There appears to be something more at work than race-specific considerations. Evans' explanation still holds substantially true:

> Black voters are realistic enough to vote for what is in their best interest. And what is in their best interest is to vote for their landlords and employers. In both cases that is the Labour Party.[32]

It is to the Labour Party that we now turn.

Notes

1. Mrs Thatcher, interviewed by Gordon Burnswith for 'World in Action', 30 January, 1978, cited in Zig-Layton Henry, 'Race and the Thatcher Government', in Layton Henry and Rich (eds), *Race, Government and Politics*, Macmillan, London 1986.
2. Nicholas Wapshott and George Brock, *Thatcher*, Futura Books, London 1983, p. 156, cited in Layton-Henry, 1986, *op cit*.
3. Zig Layton-Henry, 1986, *op cit*, p. 74.
4. David Butler and Denis Cavanagh, *The British General Election of 1987*, Macmillan, London 1988, p. 4.
5. Interview with James Goodsman, 14 June 1990.
6. *Hansard*, 1981, Vol.8, Col.1313, cited in John Solomos, *Race and Racism in*

Contemporary Britain, Macmillan, London 1989, pp. 119-20.

7. Solomos, *op cit*, p. 105.

8. See FitzGerald, *Political Parties and Black People, op cit.*, pp. 70-75

9. Interview with John Taylor, 6 February 1988.

10. Interview with James Goodsman, *op. cit.*

11. FitzGerald, *Political Parties and Black People, op cit.*, p. 22.

12. *Ibid*, p. 70-71.

13. Interview with Joyce Sampson, 20 April 1990.

14. Quoted in *The Guardian*, 4 December 1990.

15. Interview with Nirj Deva, 11 February 1988.

16. Interview with John Taylor, 6 February 1988.

17. Muhammad Anwar, *Race and Politics*, Tavistock Publications, London 1986, pp. 102-3.

18. Interview with John Taylor, 19 April 1990.

19. Interview with James Goodsman, *op. cit.*

20. *The Sunday Times*, 9 December 1990.

21. *New York Times*, 6 December 1990.

22. *Sunday Times*, 9 December 1990.

23. *Glasgow Herald*, 11 December 1990.

24. Interview with Roy Evans, 20 June 1990.

25. Liberal Party, *Inner City Disturbances*, London 1981. See also, Anwar, *op. cit.*, pp. 90-1.

26. Ivor Crewe and Bo Sarlvik, 'Partisan Dealignment in Britain 1964-1974', *British Journal of Political Science*, Vol.VII, 1977.

27. Anwar, *op. cit.*, p. 91.

28. *The Guardian*, 23.10.72, cited in Anwar, *op. cit*, p. 103.

29. Commission for Racial Equality, *Ethnic Minorities and the General Election of 1983*, London 1984.

30. Interview with Roy Evans, *op cit*.

31. *Ibid*.

32. *Ibid*.

4 The Labour Party

Class is the fundamental reason. Not that the Labour Party has a very
good record on race relations issues. It may be marginally better than
the other political parties, but it doesn't have a good record.
Nevertheless, in terms of the class issues and the common issues for
working-class people like decent housing, wages and health, the Party
represents their best interest ... It is a calculation that the Labour Party
will be more in black people's interests than a vote for any other party.
                                                           – Linda Bellos

Black political development in Britain has been intricately linked to
the Labour Party. While some black people do affiliate to other
political parties, the vast majority of black Britons have identified
more closely with the Labour Party. In both image and ideology,
they feel that their interests are served best by the Labour Party,
irrespective of whether they actually vote or their lack of official
Party membership. The overwhelming allegiance of black people to
the Labour Party would lead one to believe that a 'natural' alliance
existed between them. In the 1979 and 1983 general elections, the
Commission for Racial Equality estimated that as much as 86 per
cent and 81 per cent respectively of the black vote went to Labour,
although this survey was not based on a completely representative
sample, with some over-representation of the working class.[1] While
the figures have varied considerably from survey to survey, even
the lowest estimates put black support for the Labour Party at 64
per cent – far higher than Labour support in any other group for
which data is available. The corollary of this is that black voters are
far more loyal to the Labour Party than its traditional supporters –
the white working class who abandoned Labour in great numbers in
both the 1983 and 1987 general elections.

Why Labour?

The reasons why black people support the Labour Party are as
complicated as they are numerous. Most political commentators
cite historical, occupational and geographical links between black
migrants and Labour as the primary motives. Indeed, tradition is a
strong motivating force in voting behaviour and the black
communities have historically voted Labour. Asian activists point to
Labour's support for Indian Independence as cause for their
loyalty, while Afro-Caribbeans associate their support for the
Labour Party in Britain with the Labour Parties they voted for back
home.

> Though the Labour Parties in the West Indies were not the same as
> Labour in Britain, we saw similarities in the ideologies – the same kind
> of belief in socialism and the working class so with that kind of tradition
> it was quite natural for us to continue to support Labour.[2]

Although some black migrants came to Britain with a predeter-
mined allegiance to the labour movement, still others point to the
settlement patterns of ethnic minorities as the real cause for black
support for Labour. Geographically, ethnic minorities settled in
inner cities that were most often run by Labour-controlled local
authorities and which elected Labour MPs. Support for Labour
became a means of survival for blacks as the delivery of vital goods
and services were determined by those in the Labour Party. Black
support for Labour, therefore, was seen partly as a matter of
political expediency.

> However relatively sympathetic or hostile the main parties might have
> been to black people in principle, in practice it was with the Labour
> Party that alliances had to be forged and relationships struck and
> cultivated.[3]

If the ties between the black community and the Labour Party were
in some ways inevitable, Hilary Wainwright also suggests that the
relationship was reciprocal, though hierarchical in nature.

> In certain constituencies a pyramid of reciprocal understanding and
> relationship grew up. At the top was the MP, with power to get people
> through immigration, and to put pressure on the local council for
> housing, employment, and planning permission, and at the bottom
> were Asian families, powerless and dependent. In the middle were

Asian leaders who had power partly through their access to the MP or the council and who maintained this access partly by their ability to 'deliver' significant sections of the Asian community as votes.[4]

In other words, a system of patronage is at work – the patron being the Labour Party, its clients the black communities. The distinction between the two main non-white communities must be made here since there are significant differences in the political attitudes and the intensity of commitment towards the Labour Party between Asians and Afro-Caribbeans. Although broad generalisations about black political behaviour are problematic, the evidence tends to show that among both ethnic groups, black people do not vote Labour because of Labour's special treatment of ethnic minorities but rather because of class interest. A 1983 Harris Research Centre survey polling 258 Afro-Caribbeans and 354 Asians who always or usually voted Labour asked, 'Why do you normally vote Labour?' As the results from Table 4.1 reveal, 76 per cent of Afro-Caribbeans and 64 per cent of Asians gave their reason for Labour support as being because Labour 'supports the working class'.

Table 4.1

Reasons for Normally Voting Labour

	Asians intending to vote %				Afro-Caribbeans intending to vote %			
	All	Con	Lab	Alli.	All	Con	Lab	Alli.
They support the working class	64	50	65	57	76	50	78	50
They support blacks and Asians	31	33	34	7	7	25	7	–
Because you don't want a Conservative government	8	–	8	14	9	–	10	50
	(Base 354 usual Labour voters)				(Base 258)			

Source: Harris Survey for Black-on-Black/Eastern Eye Election Special, May 1983.

Alternatively, only 7 per cent of Afro-Caribbeans and 31 per cent of Asians said because Labour 'supports blacks and Asians'. These results imply that 'race' is not the *major* factor in black voting patterns. Blacks, like whites, tend to base their electoral choices primarily on a party's image, rather than its social or economic policies, and least of all on the party's 'race' policies (see Table 4.2). It was Labour's image as the party of the working class which seems initially to have inspired black support.

Table 4.2

Basis for electors' opinions of parties

%	Afro-Caribbeans %		Asians %		Whites	
	Con	Lab	Con	Lab	Con	Lab
General 'image'	65	66	60	58	75	65
Social policy	22	16	25	9	18	10
Economic policy	30	17	34	25	26	14
'Race' policies	2	7	4	4	0	0

(Respondents gave various reasons for their views, so column totals exceed 100 per cent.)

Source: 1984 GLC Political Attitudes Survey.

In 1979 data pooled from pre-election surveys revealed that ethnic minorities even from the middle and upper classes gave their support to the Labour Party (see Table 4.3). This clearly suggests that black support for Labour cuts across class lines, while white support for Labour is more closely correlated to their socio-economic class. The table shows that Labour voting was higher among professional and non-manual black voters than among its traditional supporters – the white working class.

Further complicating this information is a 1984 GLC survey which revealed that black respondents were less prepared to accept class labels than whites. When asked, 'Which class do you belong to?', 30 per cent of the Afro-Caribbeans and 44 per cent of the Asians responded 'Not applicable/don't know/ disapprove of class label'. Only 23 per cent of white respondents expressed their disapproval of class labelling.[5] The fact that the majority of ethnic minorities vote Labour calls into question membership of or identification with 'the working class' as the sole explanation for Labour's black support. There is some evidence that as more blacks become upwardly mobile, they are still affected by certain issues

Table 4.3

1979 General Election
Voting by Social Class within Ethnic Groups (%)

	Con	Lab	Lib	Non-Voter	(N)
White					
A,B,C	57	20	9	15	(3588)
C	40	35	5	20	(3290)
D,E	32	38	5	25	(3145)
Afro-Caribbean					
A,B,C_1	17	41	7	35	(29)
C_2	11	49	8	32	(37)
D,E	15	48	3	35	(40)
Asian					
A,B,C_1	25	42	6	28	(36)
C_2	28	50	3	19	(32)
D,E	25	50	0	25	(40)

Source: Gallup Pre-Election Surveys, 1979.

that they feel are more likely to be addressed best by the Labour Party.

Certainly, the Conservative Party's image of being tough on issues such as race relations, immigration and public spending have served as a major deterrent to black support. A 1987 Harris poll showed that 55 per cent of all black people disapproved of the Tory government's record on race, compared with 24 per cent who approved. Among Afro-Caribbeans, the number disapproving was as high as 76 per cent.[6] As one black Labour councillor put it:

> If you've got two evils ... invariably you will chose the one that is less threatening, less damaging. That's why you'll find the vast majority of black people in this country will place their political franchise with the Labour Party ... In comparison, the Tory Party personifies old colonial values, inequalities and injustices that are in the experience of black people for generations. Faced with that, there really is no choice.'[7]

This would explain why many upper- and middle-class blacks tended to vote Labour. Race may not, therefore, be the most significant factor in the black electorate's choices, but it may act as a deterrent against choosing one of the other party political alternatives.

The combined influence of class and race have long sustained black loyalty to the Labour Party, often in spite of Labour's inconsistent and far from honourable record on race relations. Labour's ambivalence towards its ever-loyal black support seems set to continue with the mounting pressure of electoral respectability bearing down on the Labour leadership. The dual imperative to attract back its white working-class and retain its black support has placed Labour in a precarious position. On the other hand, Labour strategists must take into account the very real fact that throughout the turbulent 1980s, black people continued to be the most reliable of Labour supporters. The importance of black voters, especially in inner city areas, cannot be underestimated. As Marian FitzGerald has pointed out, statistically the average Labour constituency in inner London has a black population of 23 per cent, compared to only 12 per cent in non-Labour seats. The contrast is even more dramatic in outer London constituencies where the Labour Party holds considerably fewer seats. In 1984 Labour seats averaged 22 per cent black population and those held by other parties only 9 per cent.[8] Just how Labour will respond to the challenge of maintaining this level of black support depends largely on how effective blacks are in placing their demands on the Party, and on how far the Party in turn is willing to be seen pandering to black concerns.

Little attention had been paid to the importance of the black electorate prior to the Community Relations Commission report following the two general elections of 1974. Although it now appears that the report's findings exaggerated the significance of 'ethnic marginal constituencies', it was highly successful in alerting all the political parties to the potential impact of the black vote. So by the mid-1970s the Labour Party too began to adopt a much higher profile with regard to race issues. The Labour leadership made direct appeals to recruit and retain black support. After the defeat in the general election of 1979, the National Executive Committee (NEC) circulated a memorandum to its constituency parties entitled, 'Labour and the Black Electorate', openly encouraging the Constituency Labour Parties (CLPs) to get more black people involved and admitting its reluctance in the past:

> In spite of the Party's long-standing commitment to anti-racism we have, so far, failed to convince black people that we deserve their active support. Instead, they have increasingly been organising politically into self-help and pressure groups, largely spurning mainstream party politics. Indeed, many black people – especially the youngest members of the community – are openly suspicious of the Party ... We must review our policies as they affect the ethnic minorities so that they are more relevant to their needs and offer a much more welcoming posture throughout the party.[9]

While the response to the circular was weak, it did represent a major effort on the part of the leadership to improve Labour's image. Then Shadow Home Secretary, Roy Hattersley even publicly rescinded his support for the 1968 Immigration Act. Initiatives were made on all levels within the Party to make Labour more 'relevant' to black people. The efforts ranged from policy initiatives, such as 'positive action' measures, to actively campaigning for 'black' causes. Although these efforts had varying degrees of success, some are worth noting.

In 1975 the Labour Race Action Group (LRAG) was set up as a pressure group within the Party. The main success of the Race Action Group was in disseminating pertinent information on political issues regarding race. It addressed important topics such as policing and the under-involvement of blacks in the Party, as well as advised on the formulation of anti-racist policies, particularly in Labour-controlled local authorities. Even before the NEC's 1980 circular, the Labour Race Action Group produced a leaflet to all CLPs entitled, 'Don't Take Black Votes for Granted'. The LRAG was prototypical of a succession of anti-racist advisory/pressure groups that sprang up within the Labour Party during the late 1970s and early 1980s. Many CLPs and regional Labour Parties formed anti-racist committees to address racial concerns. Not surprisingly, London was the centre of the most active participation.

In the early 1980s the London Labour Party formed the Standing Conference Against Racism (SCAR), which provided a forum for members of the black communities and delegates from CLPs to discuss and recommend initiatives on issues relevant to black people. As with similar efforts, the effectiveness of SCAR was short-lived. What started as a great idea eventually fizzled out, as its membership no longer reflected its commitment and its recommendations were given less credence.

One of the most high-profile Labour responses to the concerns of black people in this period came in the operations of the now-defunct Greater London Council (GLC). The Labour-controlled authority established a very close relationship with the black communities in London. Generally black activists viewed the GLC as a positive presence and exemplary of the kind of relationship they hoped Labour would cultivate nationally. The GLC provided research, grant-aid and consultation to black communities, under the auspices of its Ethnic Minorities Committee. In addition, the GLC pursued racial equality policies within its own employment practices and those of its education authority, ILEA. Perhaps its most useful function was in the provision of grant-aid to a wide range of black community initiatives. The highlight of the GLC's efforts was the declaration of 1984 as the 'GLC Anti-Racist Year' and the numerous activities it entailed. Despite the controversy surrounding it, the GLC promoted overall a favourable impression of the Labour Party, especially within the black community. This is probably one of the underlying reasons the GLC came under attack and was eventually abolished by the Conservative Government in 1986. Black groups were active in the campaign to save the GLC, acknowledging the strides it had made towards greater equality.

At the same time, pressure was mounting for change within the Labour Party's own structures. The movement for Black Sections in the Labour Party which began in 1983 came about as a direct response to black demands for greater representation and participation in the Party. It was a campaign for, among other things, constitutional recognition, mirroring the Women's and Youth Sections already in existence. The controversy over Black Sections was the subject of an ongoing debate within the Labour Party until 1990, despite its defeat in six successive Party conferences. In a compromise designed to settle once and for all this fractious dispute, the Labour Party finally approved a resolution that called for the establishment of a black socialist society at the 1990 Party Conference.

The National Executive Committee reacted to demands for Black Sections initially by establishing a working party to investigate black under-involvement and to make recommendations to the Party. As the movement gained momentum, members of the Labour leadership publicly began to voice their opposition, even before the working party had presented its recommendations. When the working party finally submitted its report in June 1985 and argued in favour of the principle of Black Sections, the NEC immediately sought a compromise. The net result was the establishment of a Black and Asian Advisory Committee composed of black Labour Party members selected from trade unions, local and regional constituency parties in conjunction with representatives of the NEC. A new officer was also appointed whose duties included serving the advisory committee and consulting the local constituency parties on the best ways of improving race relations and on how to monitor progress within the Party. Many black activists, and in particular the members of the Black Sections lobby, viewed this compromise as unsatisfactory, hence the continued proliferation of 'unofficial' Black Sections in CLPs that followed its announcement.

A pattern began to emerge from these early Labour responses to black people which still persists today. First, initiatives by the Labour Party have been largely reactive rather than pro-active. Second – even when spurred or shamed into action – the Labour Party has usually responded bureaucratically. The Party's first instinct has generally been the formation of 'committees', 'subcommittees', 'working parties' and other bureaucratic structures. These organisations have served as 'buffers' – creating the illusion of progress while keeping the issues out of the mainstream of decisive action. Their functions have usually been investigative and advisory. Seldom have these solutions been pro-active – encouraging the active participation of the wider black community and prompting action from the Labour Party as a whole, rather than relegating it to a dusty committee. In a similar vein, many black activists have claimed that Party's gestures towards them have been patronising in that they have sought to perpetuate a culture of dependency. In Labour's past efforts to become more 'relevant' to the black community, the Party, they argue, has relied on 'hand-out' tactics, offering 'special provisions' for blacks that foster a sense of indebtedness for the Party's 'benevolence'.

The great danger with Labour's approach to black people is that too often the Party fails to distinguish between rhetorical and actual solutions. 'For many', FitzGerald notes, 'the commitment to racial equality is a matter of self-image rather than political urgency and their active anti-racist phase was in some degree a matter of fashion.' The misconception lies in the Party's failure to 'understand that holding a consciously anti-racist policy position does not necessarily guarantee freedom from unconscious racism.'[10]

On the contrary, the Labour Party has had a less than illustrious record on race issues. One need only be reminded of the hard-line stance on immigration taken by Labour governments. Indeed, the party has proven to be much more amenable to the concerns of black people while out of office, than when it was in government. In the aftermath of the Wilson and Callaghan years, Hilary Wainwright claimed that 'racism spread like a fungus throughout the Party. It was their policy for immigration control in particular which made racism seem somehow 'official'.'[11] Labour's policy on immigration, under Wilson, became 'a matter of electoral expediency rather than political principle. This meant, in effect, outflanking the Conservatives in the expression and encouragement of racialist prejudice'.[12] Former Minister, Richard Crossman admitted the illiberalism of the Party's policies during this period, explaining that Labour felt it had to 'out-trump the Tories' and in doing so 'transforming their policy into a bipartisan policy'.[13]

It seems that Labour's response to black people has always been haunted by its fear of losing white voters. Such concerns are not entirely ill-founded, considering the past success of far-right groups like the British National Party and the National Front in targeting Labour voters. The National Front, for example, at its peak in the 1970s garnered over 10 per cent of the vote in 11 London Labour-held constituencies during a GLC election.[14] Even with the decline of explicitly racist ultra-nationalist fringe parties, the Labour Party's attitude towards black people has been and probably will continue to be overshadowed by this element of vulnerability. While the Party has considered the black vote to be a priority, problems engendered by this contradiction at the heart of Labour's support remain. As a result, ethnic minorities continue to receive mixed signals from the Labour Party. Nevertheless, viewing their interests – and those of black people generally – as best served by Labour, numerous black activists have joined the Party to seek social and political change, as much *within* as without the Party structure.

Black Involvement in the Labour Party

The growth of the black population, and its concentration, has had a significant impact on both black participation in the Labour Party and on their electoral importance to Labour. In 1971, for example, there were only eighteen constituencies where ethnic minorities made up 15 per cent or more of the population. Birmingham-Ladywood had the highest NCWP concentration with 29.2 per cent of its population being black. By 1981, the number of constituencies with 15 per cent or more black population had risen to 51 with the highest proportion being 45.7 per cent in Brent South. More significantly, in the 1983 and 1987 elections 33 of these seats were held by Labour and only 18 by the Conservatives.[15] Although a substantial black presence does not directly translate into more black political involvement, it does have some important implications. While few CLPs have made overt special efforts to recruit black members, black activism in the Labour Party has enjoyed a higher profile in areas with large black populations. Certainly, black involvement is spurred by a greater sense of 'investment' in those areas – a feeling that they have a stake in the policies that affect their communities, so that working within the Party structure would give them that voice.

However, this is only part of the story: black membership in the

Labour Party has been hindered by the same factors that hampers black political participation more generally. Their socio-economic status is one basic deterrent. It appears highly unlikely that black political involvement will ever include significantly high proportions of its population as long as black people remain economically deprived. The lack of economic resources combined with the effects of racism almost predetermines that black people will be under-involved in party politics.

It is hard to know exactly how many black people are members of the Labour Party since such statistics are not collected. What becomes apparent, however, is that the minority of blacks who do participate in party politics are atypical of black people generally.[16] Verba, Nie and Kim conducted a study of political participation in seven countries and observed that community activism tended to be just as middle-class, if not more so, as party activism. They found that the rift between 'community activist' and 'the community' was at least as great as, if not greater than, that which existed between the politicians and their electorate.[17] This suggests that even black activists who choose to participate outside Party structures are as likely to be 'atypical' of the black population at large as black party members. Moreover, given the disproportionately working-class composition of the black communities, it can be argued that black political activists are probably more atypical of their community than their white counterparts. The perceived gap between black activists and black communities has made them sensitive and vulnerable to criticism from various quarters that they are 'unrepresentative'; somehow the same problem for white politicians is less contentious and altogether less visible.

Despite such difficulties, the 1980s witnessed a dramatic increase in the number of black Labour councillors. The Greater London area provides the best example. By 1986 London boasted approximately 80 black Labour councillors out of about 87 black councillors elected in total.[18] Black people also obtained important leadership positions within the local authorities. In the 1980s again, four black people served as leaders of Labour-controlled authorities: Bernie Grant was the first black Labour Council leader when he was elected leader in Haringey in 1984; Merle Amory and Linda Bellos followed suit when they were elected in 1986 as leaders in Brent and Lambeth, respectively; Brent retained a black leader when Dorman Long was elected to replace Merle Amory who resigned in 1988. Despite the encouragement offered by this progress, the harsh reality was that by 1990 there were no longer any sitting black leaders. Grant stepped down in 1987 to run as the Labour parliamentary candidate in Tottenham. Both Amory and Bellos resigned in 1988 under adverse circumstances. Dorman Long, while the sitting leader in Brent, was deselected by his ward for the May 1990 local elections. Though ultimately reselected by another ward, he lost his position as leader of the council. Such high turnover among high-level black officials suggests the aggravated nature of the problems black politicians confront when functioning in the British political arena.

No less arduous was the task undertaken by the four MPs. Their success, in part, was a reflection of the growing number of black parliamentary candidates. The number grew from five in the 1979 election to eighteen in 1983, to 27 black parliamentary candidates in 1987. Out of the 27 black people in the 1987 general election, fourteen were Labour candidates. Recently, however, this marked increase in black political representation has not maintained its momentum. The prospects for the 1990s are not encouraging, in comparison to the relative success of the previous decade.

Competing Loyalties

Loyalty to the Labour Party for black members often conflicts with the expectations placed on them by their own communities. For black elected officials, the tension between the two is especially intense. Diane Abbott commented:

> People from the Caribbean particularly have this notion of Messianic politicians, that will deliver them to the promised land. If you look at the politicians they have had in the Caribbean, they are characterised by these enormously charismatic types ... That's all very well, but it leads to a certain passivity in black people's approach to politics.[19]

Black politicians are equally susceptible to being labelled 'sell-outs', insinuating that somehow they have 'assimilated'. The irony is that while the black communities place high expectations on these black political activists, they almost expect them to fail, as Russell Profitt, a black councillor and three times parliamentary candidate, complained: 'Black people are so used to failure, if you're a success they can't believe you're one of them anymore. They so desperately want to trust you to stand up for them, they end up distrusting you for fear of being disappointed.'[20] Russell Profitt identified a kind of defeatism:

> As a black community, we tend to want to demolish our own heroes and heroines before they are even established ... It's just tradition. If you study black history, you will see we are terribly good at demolishing our own representatives. We are not so good at giving support where it needs to be given.[21]

As black party activists walk this tightrope of competing loyalties, they also have to face isolation and exclusion within the Labour Party which nevertheless expects loyalty from its black activists. The most common complaint of black activists is that they are often expected only to deal with 'black' issues and are excluded from the discussion of other issues outside of race. Viewed as one dimensional in scope, their value is only in offering a black perspective. Some activists even see their presence as little more than a sign of tokenism.

But the uncomfortable reality for most black politicians is that they are largely dependent on the willingness of white people to support them. There are few wards in Britain where black people make up the majority, and even then black politicians cannot guarantee victory. Because of the British electoral system, minority groups are almost always 'squeezed' in this way. A first-past-the-post system based on single member constituencies ensures that the dominant group rules absolutely. Thus black people may constitute a useful section of support, but they do not have enough clout to set agendas or nominate leaders. Likewise, black people do not comprise significant numbers within the Labour Party. Fulfilling the demands of black members is thus at the discretion of their white comrades. The crude fact is that the success of black Party activists is largely dependent on the alliances they make with white people – although of course they do have some political weight, since, as has been argued, they are an important *element* in many constituencies. When black people do win political office, clearly they are representing an alliance of forces; however, this fact is often overlooked by their colleagues in the Labour Party. As Paul Boateng described:

> We are all elected to serve and represent the whole community, black and white alike. And we are accountable to both. It is important that we don't see black politicians as silhouettes – one dimensional cardboard cut-outs whose only concerns are with black issues ... Overcoming that stereotype is perhaps the hardest.[22]

While some black activists stress their accountability to both communities, others insist that issues that concern ethnic minorities are the same as those that affect the society at large. Diane Abbott argued this line:

> The concerns which black people voice about service delivery, housing, unemployment and security are important to white people as well. I don't think that providing good education and decent housing are marginal issues. The black agenda is not a marginal agenda. The black agenda goes to the heart of the political concerns facing this country ... How do you generate real equality? What should be our relationship with the third world? How do we fight apartheid? Those are very essential questions and I don't believe that they are marginal issues– or only of interest to black people.[23]

Russell Profitt even suggested that black people are the best qualified to articulate these shared concerns, since most black elected officials disproportionately represent deprived inner city areas. Adding, however, to these pressures of rival loyalties and the threat of marginalisation is the omnipresent and pervasive problem of racism that forever circumscribes the experience of black people in party politics.

Although Labour has an image of being more liberal on 'race' than the other parties, it is far from free of racial prejudice. While the Labour Party espouses an anti-racist rhetoric, its actions have at times conveyed the opposite impression. The 1968 Immigration Act was brought in by a Labour Government to prevent the entry of Kenyan Asians carrying British passports. And the 1981 Nationality Act brought in by a Tory Government was not very different from the previous Labour administration's Green Paper on the same subject. This is firm evidence of Labour's tarnished record on anti-racism. 'We have not deluded ourselves into thinking that the Labour Party is somehow free of racism', Phil Sealy, former Lambeth councillor, insisted. 'All the change we have had has not come because of the Labour Party, it has come *despite* the Labour Party'.[24] David Upshal, a black journalist, has argued that the Labour leadership is caught in an 'Anti-Racist dilemma' in which they often want to address the concerns of black people, but their ability actually to deliver far-reaching reform is hampered by its perceived electoral liability.[25]

The experience of some black members is that sections of the white working class, Labour's traditional supporters, tend to be more overtly racist than their middle class counterparts. In direct competition with black workers for jobs, housing and wages, white workers often feel threatened. In many ways, they are the ones who stand to gain most by racial discrimination. Jonathan Hall, former Press Officer for Brent South Labour Party, conceded:

> The working class can be the most unsympathetic toward ethnic minorities. Just look at tabloid papers that are targeted towards the white working class, like the *Sun* and *News of the World*, that profess to reflect and articulate their views. They are often blatantly racist ... This poses a big problem for us [the Labour Party] because here you have the Labour leadership making promises to blacks, yet among its own structures there are powerful forces in the form of trade unions that have these racist people in them.[26]

It is unfair, however, to place racism within the Labour Party solely at the doorstep of the white working class. All the evidence suggests that no socio-economic class is exempt from some form of conscious or unconscious racism. Some black political activists argue that middle-class racism is the hardest to handle. Linda Bellos declared:

> When a white working-class person is being racist, you can deal with that. You know their language ... you know what they are saying and you can even understand partly why they say it ... What is hard to deal with is middle-class racism ... When somebody uses a lot of very fine language to make sure that you don't get the job, there's nothing to confront. The reason you're not getting the job is actually because you're black but they're telling you it's not. There's nothing you can confront.[27]

White liberals who see themselves ideologically in the same camp as blacks, it is suggested, can be the most dangerous. Identifying with the left of the Labour Party, they are the ones who truly believe they are anti-racist and are unaware of their own domineering and patronising behaviour. Once again, it is the controversy over black sections which has become the *locus classicus* of all these problems:

> The Labour Party opposes black sections because any argument for their necessity implies that the Party has been operated on a basis which discriminates against black people. The dilemma is clearly exposed: well-intentioned, good anti-racist socialists find it hard to admit their inadequacies.[28]

The reality for many black Party members was that they felt that many of their demands and needs had not been met by the Party at large. Frustrated by their experiences within the Party's obfuscatory bureaucracy, some black members sought to take matters into their own hands. The campaign for black sections in the Labour Party, with its principle of self-organisation, represented a pivotal point in black participation in British politics. The seven-year debate and what appears to be its final resolution are the subject of the following chapter.

Notes

1. Marian FitzGerald, *Political Parties and Black People, op cit.*, p.12.
2. Interview with Phil Sealy, 10 March 1988.
3. Marian FitzGerald, *Black People and Party Politics in Britain*, Runnymede Trust, London 1987, pp.20-1.
4. Hilary Wainwright, *Labour: A Tale of Two Parties*, Hogarth Press, London 1987, pp.192-3.
5. Marian FitzGerald, 1987, *op.cit.*, p.13.
6. *Political Attitudes Survey*, Harris Research Centre, London May 1987.
7. Interview with Andrew Carnegie, 25 February 1988.
8. FitzGerald, 1984, *op.cit.*, p.33.
9. 'Labour and the Black Electorate', Labour Party (NEC Committees on Home Affairs and Organisation), London, February 1980.
10. FitzGerald, 1984, *op.cit.*, p.32.
11. Wainwright, *op.cit.*, p.189.
12. *Ibid.*, p.190.
13. *Ibid.*
14. FitzGerald, 1984, *op.cit.*, p.30.
15. Zig Layton-Henry, 'Black Electoral Participation: An Analysis of Recent Trends', in H. Goulbourne (ed), *Black Politics in Britain*, Avery, Aldershot 1990, p.27.

16. FitzGerald, 1984, *op cit*, p.106.

17. Cited in FitzGerald, *ibid*.

18. Zig Layton-Henry and Donley T. Studlar, 'The Electoral Participation of Black and Asian Britons: Integration or Alienation?', Parliamentary Affairs, Vol.38, Summer 1985, p.314.

19. Interview with Diane Abbott, 25 February 1988.

20. Quoted in FitzGerald, 'The Emergence of Black Councillors and MPs in Britain', Conference Paper, November 1987, p.11.

21. Interview with Russell Profitt, 11 February 1988.

22. Interview with Paul Boateng, June 1987.

23. Interview with Diane Abbott, *op.cit.*

24. Interview with Phil Sealy, 10 March 1988.

25. David Upshal, 'The Labour Party: An Anti-Racist Dilemma', *New Socialist*, December 1987, pp.36-7.

26. Interview with Jonathan Hall, 25 February 1988.

27. Interview with Linda Bellos, 14 March 1988.

28. Quoted by David Upshal, *op.cit.*, p.37.

5   The Campaign for Black Sections

Black representation is a cause whose time has come. We are moving from protest to politics. We are moving from protest to power.[1]
— Bill Morris

During the October 1990 Party conference, Labour adopted a proposal which called for the setting up of a single affiliated organisation for its members of African, Caribbean and Asian descent, with local and regional groups and direct representation on the National Executive Committee. The adoption of Composite 8 brought to an end the seven year long battle waged by black Labour activists for formal recognition of their right to self-determination and representation within the Party. Although the resolution did not bring the 'Black Sections' which the campaigners initially envisaged, it was nevertheless greeted as a hard-won victory for the principle of autonomous black organisation within the Party. As the Black Socialist Society is still a relatively new organisation, it is worth looking back on the movement which brought it about and examining its significance as a catalyst for black representation in Britain.

The Raison d'Etre of Black Sections

The Black Sections campaign was essentially the product of the growth in black activism in the Labour Party during the late 1970s. As more black people joined Labour during this time (when all the political parties were beginning to courting the black vote), black activists seized the opportunity to make their own demands and to influence the party's politics. The initial idea from which the campaign eventually emerged was conceived by Ben Bousquet, Billy Poh and Ray Philbert in May 1982. According to Bousquet, a councillor in the London Borough of Kensington and Chelsea and a veteran community activist, the original plan was to organise a 'mass grassroots movement which would encompass all black people and cut across political parties'.

The desire for a mass black movement was in part a response to the riots of 1981, but more specifically, it was a recognition of the frustration black Britons felt with the political system. 'Blacks were getting nowhere fast, so we wanted to organise this mass black movement', Bousquet explained. 'It was going to last only two years and give one quick jolt to black politics. It was supposed to be a grassroots movement and was to affect every aspect of black life'.[2] This early conception proved impossible to co-ordinate as grassroots activists were often too dispersed and busy in their local communities to organise nationally. But as black activists joined forces with Labour's left, the movement gained more credence as a campaign that could be waged within the Labour Party.

The Labour Party was, after all, the Party that had the most direct impact on the the day-to-day lives of black people. In that respect, most black activists did not view the limitation of the movement to an intra-Labour Party campaign as a disadvantage. Former chair of Black Sections, Marc Wadsworth, explained why the movement was founded in the Labour Party:

> Many of the local areas that affect black people are Labour authorities. So we could either be a participant or an observer – a powerless observer. And we are not about being powerless observers. The Black Sections movement [was] about getting in and demanding the empowerment of our communities. If Labour authorities control them, then we want to make sure we have our hand on the control lever. That's our reason for being in the Labour Party. The Labour Party has power and we will be where the power is – unashamedly.[3]

In fact, two inter-related developments within the Labour Party combined with the pressure from black activists to create the conditions for the Black Sections movement: the demand for greater democracy and the rise of factionalism within the Party. The campaign for democratic reform and constitutional change in the late 1970s and early 1980s, which resulted, for example, in the mandatory re-selection of MPs, lent both legitimacy and a real political lever to black activists' demand for enhanced representation.

The second condition which created a more conducive political atmosphere for intra-party campaigning was the proliferation of ideological factions and groupings within the Party from both the left and the right. The Tribune Group, the Labour Race Action Group, the Socialist Educational Association, and the Campaign for Labour Party Democracy were just a few examples. Black Party members were active participants in many of the new left-wing groups. In fact, it was through the Labour Party Race Action Group that the first model resolution in 1983 was circulated for Party conference: the momentum for black representation within the Party had begun.

The existence of other 'Sections' in the Labour Party served as a precipitating factor. 'How could they deny us the right to organise, when there [were] women's sections and youth sections, even the Jewish Party members have an organised pressure group?' asked Diane Abbott, an early activist in the Black Sections movement.[4] The motivating rationale for the campaign was, therefore, that black voters formed an equally important constituency, and that the Party needed to be rendered more accountable to their needs as well.

The central objective of the movement was to secure constitutional recognition by the Party with the same privileges and amenities enjoyed by the Women's and Youth Sections. They demanded official representation at every level of the party, especially the right to nominate and select their own candidates for council and parliamentary seats. Besides the power to short-list, the campaign also insisted on having a seat reserved on the National Executive Committee (NEC) of the Labour Party for their own representative. The bottom line for Black Section activists was participation and representation *with autonomy*.

The movement provided the platform for making 'race-specific' demands and thus imposed a 'black perspective' on the traditional class-based political agenda of the Party. Linda Bellos, a former national treasurer of the Black Sections, claims a wider significance for the campaign than simply its effect on the Labour Party:

> We raised race as a political issue, but on our own terms as a positive thing. By showing we are here to stay and these are the things that we declare will stop the discrimination we experience, all the political parties have been forced to respond.[5]

In promoting black representation, the movement also insisted on racial exclusivity. Amid criticism of creating 'apartheid' within the Party, Black Sections activists argued that black representatives were the best advocates of the interests of black people. 'Only he who weareth the shoe, knoweth the pinks', Phil Sealy, former race relations advisor in Lambeth, declared. 'White people are always trying to map the road for us and they never think black people are capable of mapping their own road'.[6] Black activists also sought to avoid the problems which they felt had befallen CARD in the 1960s: they felt threatened by the prospect of their campaign being 'hijacked' by white liberals, whom they feared would side-track their efforts and distort their objectives. When confronted with the problem of defining 'black', many Black Sections members insisted that there was no problem because it was a self-definition.

Official Disapproval

Now that the controversy has largely subsided, it is easy to forget the suspicion and hostility which the demands of Black Sections campaigners provoked. The issue of Black Sections was first brought to the attention of the Labour Party during its annual Party Conference in 1983. The campaign was launched with the help of the Greater London Regional Labour Party which organised its inaugural meeting in September 1983, and by the Labour Party Race Action Group which circulated a 'model' resolution on its behalf for submission to the party conference. The 1983 proposal was included in a motion which called for the party to accept the principle of 'positive discrimination' and to make the effort to eradicate discrimination within its own structures by setting up Black Sections. This first resolution encouraged the Labour Party to recognise

> that in this unequal society there is no real equality of opportunity and that working-class people, women and ethnic minority groups suffer severe discrimination ... Our party itself is unfortunately not free from this and therefore accepts the principle of positive discrimination in favour of disadvantaged groups ... in particular the right of black members of the party to organise together in the same way as Women's Sections and Young Socialist branches.[7]

The motion was remitted before a vote could be taken. Speaking on behalf of the NEC, Jo Richardson insisted that 'our sympathies are with the aspirations which are behind the composite', but asserted that the issue of black under-involvement needed close examination with attention given to all possible proposals. She added that little advantage would be achieved at that stage for 'the NEC's hands to be tied too specifically'. As a result, the Labour Party set up a 'working party' consisting of both black and white party members to study the question of black Party participation and Richardson was made the chairperson.

While the working party deliberated, the Black Sections activists continued to organise and the Labour leadership moved into open opposition. In July 1984, the first official National Black Sections Conference was held in Birmingham and attracted close to 300 black delegates, mostly Afro-Caribbeans. As a pre-emptive strike designed to dissipate support for Black Sections, and without regard to the efforts of the working party, key members of the Labour leadership publicly and strategically voiced their disapproval. Labour leader Neil Kinnock was adamantly opposed and called Black Sections a 'cul-de-sac' taking the Labour Party 'nowhere fast'. Roy Hattersley, the deputy leader, considered them 'deeply patronising, a retrograde step'. His chief objection was that 'they divided us when we should be united'.[8] Gerald Kaufman, Shadow Home Secretary at the time, referred to Black Sections as 'some kind of ghetto' and a form of 'apartheid' within the Party.

The opposition from the leadership reflected the general concerns of many of the opponents of Black Sections. The fear of conflicts over racial definitions was voiced by Kinnock: 'I'm not going to have divisions of race ... underscored and turned into constitutional effect'.[9] A racially segregated section, he argued, would be an impediment to changing attitudes on race both within the Party and within society because it took, so he argued, responsibility for the question of racial discrimination out of the mainstream of discussion. Therefore, the move to create Black Sections was portrayed as regressive for race relations rather than as a progressive step.

The official Labour criticism was conveniently paraded under the banner of 'Party unity'. Hattersley went so far as to call Black Sections an anathema to socialism, stating that 'it is, or ought to be, an article of socialist faith that all men and women are treated the same. We can't insist on this ... if we then choose to treat the races differently within the Labour Party itself.'[10] The unity theme was highly suspect: given the growing disunity the Party was already experiencing at the hands of its hard left, placing responsibility for the divisions on Black Sections activists was more than a little disingenuous.

Of course, the real irony was that (notwithstanding the leadership's rationalisation), the Party *had* approved Women's and Youth Sections; yet it refused to recognise Black Sections on the same principle. Neil Kinnock rebutted this charge of inconsistency:

> No one could sustain the argument that history's precedent for a provision for women is parallel with racism. Black people suffer from different forms of discrimination which requires a different response. It is discrimination felt by individuals, not by mass groupings.[11]

Black people in the Labour Party could be forgiven, perhaps, for failing to understand Kinnock's distinction between women who were discriminated as a 'mass grouping' and blacks who were discriminated against merely as individuals. For some black activists this failure to acknowledge the systematic and institutional nature of racism in British society amounted to an indication of the Labour Party's own racism. 'It's out and out bloody racism,' Phil Sealy exclaimed. 'There is no other reason for the Party to provide special provisions for women and not for us.'

The acrimonious debate which ensued during the 1984 party conference showed the staunch commitment of both sides to their arguments. With the working party still out in deliberation the NEC once again asked for a remittance of the resolutions on Black Sections. Viewing this as a delaying tactic, black activists continued to press the issue. The 1984 conference agenda contained eighteen resolutions in favour of Black Sections, one opposed and seven amendments. The resolutions and amendments in favour were composited into two resolutions which were resoundingly defeated. The first composite resolution lost on a card vote of 5,427,000 to 500,000 and the second resolution in favour of Black Sections was defeated by 5,645,000 to 418,000.[12] The campaign had failed to receive the powerful bloc votes of the trade unions. Only the NUM supported the motion which, considering the distance between the

Labour leadership and the striking miners, was little consolation. Nevertheless, the black activists left the 1984 conference vowing to keep returning until they won.

The campaign continued by establishing 'unofficial' Black Sections. By the time of 1985 National Black Sections Conference in Brixton, some 24 CLPs sent delegates. Criticised for its lack of policy and for its failure to mobilise the black community, the movement made plans to shift its focus in the hope of gaining wider support. Given the factionalism which was reaching a peak within the Party at that time, the campaign moved progressively into alliance with the left.

Sharon Atkin succeeded Russell Profitt to become the second chair of Black Sections. With her ascendancy, the leadership of the movement was taken over by the Black Labour Activists Campaign (BLAC) which had formed during 1985 to 'promote left politics'. With BLAC activists at its head, as one commentator observed, 'the future direction of Black Sections was becoming clearer: alliances would be forged with the left of the Labour Party and policies would need to be developed'.[13] Some original campaigners, like Ben Bousquet and Vidya Anand (then a prospective Labour parliamentary candidate for Folkstone and Hythe), resigned over the new direction the campaign was taking. They claimed that this shift indicated that the campaign was being 'hijacked by middle-class politicians' more concerned with promoting their careers than the authentic interests of the black community.

For the three succeeding years, the campaign was controlled by black activists who identified with the hard left: the fate of Black Sections was thus bound by the success or failure of that alliance. In fact, it was this association which hastened the campaign's demise. As the leftwing of the Party declined, the movement found that its political partner had become a millstone dragging it down. The support of Scargill's NUM was of little value given their sorry defeat in the 1984-85 dispute, particularly in the light of widespread criticism of the NUM President's conduct of the strike. Moreover, the marginalisation of Bennism, and the leadership's successful crack-down on the Militant Tendency, pointed to further failure for the cause of Black Sections.

Underlying the leadership's determined disciplining of the Labour left was a desperate desire to restore the Party's electoral prospects. Amid all the analogies of creating a 'ghetto' and an 'apartheid' within the Party, the real fear of the Labour leadership was that an endorsement of Black Sections would lose them votes. The issue was a prime target for exploitation by the right-wing press and by other political parties. 'They are afraid that we might become an embarrassment to the Party', former Labour councillor, Andrew Carnegie acknowledged.[14] By its association with the 'loony left', the Black Sections campaign was seen as yet another thorn in the side of the Labour Party.

When the working party finally *did* reach a decision in the spring of 1985 to recommend the establishment of Black Sections with delegate rights at every level of the party, the Labour leadership rejected the proposal. The working party submitted two reports. A majority report in favour of Black Sections and a minority report which suggested the creation of a 'black advisory committee', designed to promote the participation of black people in the Party but without constitutional change. The NEC rejected the working party's majority recommendation on a twelve to three vote. Even before the report was submitted, Kinnock launched a public attack declaring his implacability:

> I am adamantly against Black Sections. The overwhelming majority of the NEC are against them. I would be against any development which constitutionally gave separate sections on the basis of colour of skin or ethnic origins. I would not give a damn if the whole Labour Party was against me on this. This is not the case, but it is a matter of basic values.[15]

As a compromise, the late Eric Heffer proposed to the NEC that black members be given the opportunity to organise outside the Party as an affiliated organisation. Given the eventual outcome it is ironic that Heffer's 1985 proposal for affiliated status was attacked by both the leadership and black activists. Feelings were running so high that neither side was willing to reach a compromise, and in any case Heffer's proposal, like the working party's majority recommendation, was also defeated by the NEC. Instead, the NEC opted to propose to the Party conference the establishment of a black advisory committee.

At the 1985 Labour Party Conference, the motion for Black Sections was again solidly defeated.[16] The Party voted to establish the Black and Asian Advisory Committee (BAAC) and appointed a full-time officer with the responsibility of handling 'race issues'. This compromise was far from satisfactory for Black Section activists who were calling for automatic representation at every level of the Party.

Locked in this ritual conflict, the campaign proceeded in its original form demanding constitutional recognition within the Party, and was again defeated at the 1986, 1987 and 1988 Party conferences. It was not until the 1988 conference that signs of progress towards a compromise were first evident. Rejecting once again the proposal for the establishment of Black Sections, the delegates *did* approve a motion that recognised the principle of self-determination and direct representation for black members as being essential to a democratic socialist party. It was this acknowledgement which started the negotiations between the leadership and MP Bernie Grant to reach a resolution to the controversy that both sides could accept.

Throughout the debate, black activists remained committed to the initial goals. 'There are certain basics that cannot be compromised and they are autonomy, incorporation and represen-tation ... guaranteed representation at every level', former national chair, Narendra Makenji asserted. 'We cannot accept anything that falls short of that'.[17] In the face of these defeats, black activists were always quick to claim that their real support was within the black communities. The evidence, however, suggests that this was not necessarily so. As the movement became more centrally controlled – intent on promoting its own members within the Labour Party, rather than on developing policies and organising the black communities – its grassroots support, never very strong, showed no sign of growing.

Black Support?

A 1985 Harris poll of 2,500 Afro-Caribbeans and 2,600 Asians conducted on behalf of Channel 4's programme, 'Black on Black', showed that 63 per cent of its black respondents thought that 'it is wrong for political parties to set up sections exclusively for black people', while only eighteen per cent said it was right and nineteen per cent said they didn't know.[18] By 1987, the numbers approving had increased, but still the majority rejected the idea of exclusively Black Sections. The results of another Harris survey of political attitudes in 1987 revealed that 45 per cent of all black respondents disapproved of separate sections for black people, while 33 per cent approved. Within the two largest non-white ethnic groups, just as many Afro-Caribbeans (44 per cent) as Asians (46 per cent) disapproved, dispelling the myth that Afro-Caribbeans were overwhelmingly supportive of Black Sections. Professional and managerial black people were the most disapproving, with 63 per cent expressing their objection, and only 14 per cent giving approval.[19]

It is hard to ascertain the specific causes of black opposition to Black Sections. The reasons are as complex as they are diverse. Much of the controversy, however, centered around four main criticisms of the movement: the marginalisation of black experience, middle-class careerism, lack of policy, and racial exclusivity.

'Marginalisation' became a catch-all phrase on both sides of the debate over Black Sections. Opponents contended that Black Sections marginalised black people in politics by relegating them to a small faction within the Party. They equated Black Sections with a 'ghetto' in which black activists would fight among themselves for the few political crumbs that were designated to them. Black Sections were therefore seen as a diversion from the real issues facing black people. Paul Boateng contended that, from his discussions in the black community, the complaint he heard most often was that Black Sections served only to 'marginalise' the black experience. Boateng explained:

> The majority of black people don't want Black Sections ... I've found that most blacks see it as sectarian and marginalising. Black people want to be a part of the mainstream. They don't want to be segregated by sectarian divides. They want to be more fully integrated into British society and they don't see how Black Sections achieves that goal.[20]

Proponents of Black Sections countered that black people had already been marginalised in British society and that Black Sections sought to rectify that problem. Black Sections advocates contended that they 'demarginalised' blacks by offering them a chance to participate in mainstream party politics in a more meaningful way.

They pointed to the recruitment of more black members and the increase in black political involvement since the advent of Black Sections as proof of their success. Diane Abbott maintained: 'When I joined the Labour Party black people had no presence whatsoever. Then Black Sections came along and brought more blacks into the Party. We are offering an alternative to marginalised politics.'[21] Throwing back Gerald Kaufman's words, she insisted:

> I'll tell you what is apartheid. All-white parties in multi-racial constituencies, that's apartheid. An all-white House of Commons, that's apartheid. We [Black Sections] are providing a remedy for this apartheid.[22]

Although the campaign for Black Sections has done much to raise awareness of the need for black political participation and representation, the extent to which its efforts have actually 'demarginalised' black political experience is highly questionable. The more limited, but realistic conclusion is that blacks have moved from being completely marginalised *outside* the mainstream of party politics to being relatively marginalised *within*.

While some black opponents feared that Black Sections isolated them from participating in the mainstream of the Party, others expressed their apprehension over the specific aims of Black Sections. Some black people felt that the movement's emphasis on constitutional demands was missing the point. It served only to trivialise the issue. Bill Morris, then deputy general secretary of the Transport and General Workers Union, was one of the leading black opponents of Black Sections for just this reason. He thought that the fixation with constitutional demands was 'taking us away from the real aims of the movement – the increased participation of blacks in the Party.'[23] Even Diane Abbott, avid supporter of Black Sections, expressed her initial opposition to the movement on these grounds, but changed her opinion when she witnessed the Party's response to the proposal:

> I envisaged the constitutional change would take perhaps as long as a decade to achieve and I felt this would distract from the real business of black recruitment and organisation ... I was wrong because of the reaction of white people to the campaign. At one party conference, we lined up to make our speeches and somebody at the top table said to another MP, 'What are *those people* doing in *our* Party?' It is the

reaction of white people to Black Sections that made me believe in them.[24]

While Abbott was convinced of its merit, the movement faced constant criticism from various quarters for lacking coherent policy positions.

A. Sivanandan, Director of the Institute of Race Relations, and Darcus Howe of the *Race Today* Collective, in particular, argued that the campaign failed to 'deliver' in this respect. Their suspicion was that Black Sections activists had opted to further their own political careers by channelling all their energies into political representation, rather than developing a coherent body of political strategy. *Race Today* registered in 1984 its concern over the motives of the campaign when it noted:

> The alternative to careerism is a political approach and orientation in several areas of national policy. To date not a single word has been spoken or written by black sections in this regard.[25]

Paul Sharma, a former London campaign organiser and author of the Black Sections constitution, became an outspoken critic of the direction of the movement during its last few years. He complained:

> Substance has been almost completely ignored. A minority in Black Sections are determined to lead a holy war, perpetual conflict against the Labour leadership. They have always demanded 110 per cent thereby obtaining 0 per cent. The tragedy is that all this has been done in the name of black people in our society who frankly don't give a damn whether there is a Black Section. Their concern is the delivery of policies that affect their lives.[26]

Responding to these complaints, the campaign in 1988 published *The Black Agenda*, a document outlining Black Sections' policy on issues such as education, unemployment and health. Launching the paper, the leadership announced that this was the beginning of 'phase two' of the campaign. The report from the Black Sections National Conference held in Manchester that year was that activists planned to promote the campaign's positions by circulating the policy briefs throughout Britain, and by staging discussion meetings as part of a national Black Sections lecture tour.[27] 'Phase two' of the campaign had come too late and never got off the ground; the movement had already lost its momentum.

There were still some black opponents who questioned the sincerity of those involved and suggested that the real objectives of the campaigners were self-serving. Because the campaign's major success was in increasing the awareness of the need for black representation, its supporters were often accused of furthering their own political careers 'on the back' of the legitimate interests of the black community. For all the rhetoric about a grassroots movement, the evidence suggests that, in common with most political organisations, the campaign for Black Sections operated on a 'top-down' model: those who benefitted most were the privileged few at the helm of the movement. The success of the campaign was therefore largely symbolic since the mass of black people could point only to the individual triumphs of an isolated handful of black politicians.

Black Sections advocates dismiss the charge of middle-class careerism and denounce it as a tactic to discredit any black participation in the political system. Linda Bellos pointed out the contradiction that arises when black activists play the political game:

> White people always look for a way to undermine our credibility when we try to get into politics. To call us middle-class careerists is such a contradiction. On the one hand, if we as black politicians are inarticulate then we are authentic, but if we learn their language and use their rules then they say that we are not legitimate – we don't really represent the black community. So white people win both ways around. It's just a successful means of ensuring blacks continue to be disenfranchised.[28]

While Linda Bellos is right to draw attention to the double standards operating here, the fact is that the description of the movement as middle-class does have a grounding in reality. Increasingly, those who participate in the political arena tend to be middle-class and educationally privileged, and therefore atypical of the communities they represent. The entire membership of the Labour Party has been moving in this direction, so there is little reason to expect that activists in Black Sections should be any different. In fact, there is reason to believe that the disparity between black political activists and the black community would be even greater, given the disproportionately working-class composition of black communities.

The fourth criticism of the campaign often cited by opponents was the problem of defining 'black' that arose from the campaign's stress on the political importance of black autonomy. Russell Profitt, the first national chair of Black Sections, acknowledged the salience of the problem created by the campaign's demand for exclusivity:

> The demands of black sections require people to basically associate themselves with being black. That poses a problem for a lot of people even if they are black as black can be. They tend to think that 'black' is a much too blunt approach.[29]

Although creating racial divisions is uncomfortable, Black Sections proponents insisted on its necessity. Many have argued that 'black' is a 'political colour' and that Afro-Caribbeans and Asians are united by their common experience of oppression. Others are more sceptical and suggest that there is discontent with the use of the term 'black' to encompass a variety of different non-white ethnic groups, especially among Asians. While some Asians who are politically active accept the necessity of the term 'black' as a political colour, the vast majority do not identify with the term. One British Asian academic has openly challenged the use of the word 'black' to define all ethnic minorities and suggested that Asian ethnic identities are subsumed and stifled by this usage. Dr Tariq Modood argued that Afro-Caribbeans and Asians cannot unite positively under the single label 'black' because 'peoples of Sub-Saharan African roots ... are thought to be the quintessential or exemplary cases of black consciousness ... Asians in Britain will not necessarily be capable of being black in the full sense but be only secondary or ambiguous blacks'.[30] Keith Vaz confirms that 'there is a lot of resentment by Asians to the term "black" ', although he also asserted that 'in politics it is very important that blacks and Asians are kept together ... The last thing that we need is to be divided'.[31]

Changing Tactics

By the late 1980s, both the campaigners and the Labour leadership were so entrenched in their own positions that the original issue of black participation and representation in the Party had virtually been forgotten. During the 1988 Party Conference, Labour committed itself to the principle of black self-determination, so the main contention to resolve between the two camps became what would be the best means by which to achieve this aim. With successive conference defeats and little sign of widespread external support, Black Sections activists were under great pressure to change tactics. A clear split became evident within the movement. From 1987 on, the debates on 'The Way Forward' at Black Sections annual conferences were the most lively sessions and indicated a clear division between those hardliners who stuck to the founding demands of the campaign and those who felt that other alternatives had to be explored if the movement was to progress.

Some of the movement's most visible and prominent members now began to distance themselves from the campaign. Most notably, the four black MPs, who in any event had different approaches to the issue, as previously noted, showed signs of a retreat on the issue. After their election, their position became crucial for the public profile of the Black Sections movement. At the same time, the constraints of public office meant that their public pronouncements had to be cautious, since they were representing a wider constituency; they became much more reserved and sceptical. While all four remained nominally committed to the principle of black autonomy, albeit some more strongly than others, none of them were as active in the movement as they had been before.

It is difficult to determine whether their lower profile in the campaign was attributable to their demanding new jobs as parliamentarians or whether it was indication of a new-found willingness to play the political game by the rules. At any event, as the Labour leadership clamped down on its leftward-leaning members, it became less beneficial to be associated with the Black Sections movement. The handling of Sharon Atkin's deselection in the run-up to the 1987 general election provided a perfect illustration of these new circumstances.

As prospective parliamentary candidates, the leading black activists were quick to distance themselves from Atkin's statement at the 1987 Black Sections conference in Birmingham which had caused the Party considerable embarrassment. Within days, Abbott, Boateng, Grant and Profitt, four of the major black parliamentary contenders, issued a public statement pledging their support to the Labour Party:

> Our over-riding interest is getting Labour into government. Nothing can be allowed to stand in the way of this. We think that the current argument over black sections has been blown out of proportion by a hostile media. We call on all sections of the Labour Party to set aside internal differences to concentrate all efforts on winning the general election.[32]

Those black candidates who were successful made a still clearer shift. Whilst all four black MPs had at some point spoke openly in favour of Black Sections on Party platforms prior to their election, during the 1988 conference, as MPs, when arguably their voice could have been the most effective, they remained relatively silent.[33] Aside from sitting together during the conference's debate over Black Sections, ostensibly as a gesture of symbolic solidarity, their comments after the motion's defeat revealed a marked change of tone, if not of substance. Bernie Grant told the press: 'It's clear that we cannot go on the same way. I am opposed to us coming back to conference next year and putting the same resolution.'[34] Similarly, Keith Vaz expressed his disapproval of the style and approach of Black Sections campaigning during the conference: 'If you conduct a debate sensibly, people will listen to you much more than if you shout at them.'[35] Both Vaz and Boateng became openly critical of the Black Sections leadership. Boateng remarked: 'While I am a major supporter of the constitutional demands and will continue to articulate that, I will have nothing to do with the tactics adopted by the national leadership of Black Sections. They have been appalling.'[36]

While few would deny their right to be publicly critical of the leadership of Black Sections at this time, the real tragedy was that they no longer regarded it as their responsibility to do something about the demise of the movement. Boateng insisted:

> It's not my role to change Black Sections, my role is to do the best that I can in Parliament for the constituency that I represent and if that reflects well on black MPs then so much the better.[37]

Grant was more accommodating and served as a liaison between the Black Sections campaign and the NEC in seeking a resolution to the long-running controversy. Diplomacy finally won the day when

Black Sections activists gave their mandate to considering other options in the hope of appeasing both the movement and the Party leadership. Compromise might be possible as long as the basic principle was maintained: a single unitary organisation with internal democracy and automatic representation on policy-making bodies.

Affiliation: A Black Socialist Society

The affiliated society emerged as the main alternative to Black Sections. A 1985 minority report from the working party on positive discrimination had first made mention of a national black organisation with local branches affiliated to CLPs. In expressing opposition to the working party's recommendation in favour of Black Sections, dissenters Rita Austin, Robin Corbett and Marian FitzGerald prepared a minority report in which they proposed a 'Labour Black Rights Campaign'. They urged that 'membership, as with the Socialist Education Association and other similar branches, would be determined by the political support for its aim and therefore open to all party members'.[38]

Likewise, Eric Heffer had made a similar suggestion, as a peace offering, to the NEC before the 1985 Labour Party Conference. Heffer's proposal made a point of differentiating between ethnic minorities, suggesting that 'Afro-Caribbean, Asian and African peoples' formed appropriate groups or organisations and affiliated to the Labour Party at all levels. Moreover, he argued for a completely new NEC division, instead of simply expanding the number of places on the NEC for Socialist Societies. However, this proposal was solidly defeated by the NEC in July 1985 on a sixteen to eight vote and never made it to Party conference.

The affiliated society option gained legitimacy when it received support from Bill Morris, Britain's most prominent black trade unionist, then deputy general secretary of the Transport and General Workers' Union. Morris called for the setting up of a national Black Socialist Society with the rights of nomination and representation, like other affiliated societies. He recommended that the society be based on open membership, although all elected officers and delegates would be required to be members of the Labour Party. Non-Labour members would have to be at least eligible to join the Party. Morris has also made the case for expanding the number of places for Socialist Societies on the NEC from the present single place to two or three reserved places.

Outlining this proposal in January 1988, Bill Morris argued that 'it was time for the trench warfare to stop'. 'Although it would be unkind to say that Black Sections are an idea whose time has gone,' Morris continued, 'the time has come to move on.'[39] A long-standing opponent of Black Sections, Morris admitted that 'the debate on black representation in the Labour Party has helped to give us four black MPs and to raise the Party's and the nation's consciousness of racism and discrimination'. He contended that the protest tactics of the Black Sections campaign, which he described as 'establishment tree-shaking', had become counterproductive.

The real advantage for the activists was that the proposal would, ostensibly at least, preserve the core objectives of the campaign by creating an avenue for black representation in the Party's policy-making machinery. Nevertheless, it received a mixed reaction from Black Sections activists. The national leadership of Black Sections issued a public statement acknowledging the proposal as 'a positive and welcomed contribution'. Marc Wadsworth, once the fervent defender of Black Sections, recognised the validity of the compromise: 'If powerful groups like these [trade unions] were to support any similar new proposals for black socialists capable of winning support on the NEC and at Labour Party Conferences, we would be open to persuasion'.[40] Those activists who supported the proposal for affiliation as a legitimate option did not view their approval as inconsistent with their continued support for the original campaign. As Mike Wongsam, the leader of campaign, asserted:

> We agreed that the affiliated society proposal is something we can use as the basis for discussion if it can gain wider acceptance. But obviously any proposal we accept must satisfy our own criteria: that is to say it has to accommodate black self-organisation, be unitary with its own internal democracy and must have automatic representation. This is the acid test. If the affiliated society meets these criteria, then we think it is a meaningful step towards realising black representation inside the Labour Party.[41]

The proposal still met with suspicion from the movement's

hardliners, but their defeat at 1990 Black Sections annual conference in Liverpool paved the way for the compromise proposal's adoption at Labour Party Conference in October 1990.

The conditions were finally ripe for rapprochement. The Labour Party was eager to lay the issue to rest before the next general election and sought an expedient solution that would constitutionally recognise black involvement in the Party, but in a form that would be electorally acceptable. In the interim, a new policy was also adopted which called for constitutional rule changes to be addressed by special rule revision conferences which would be held once every four years. This new policy effectively meant that the Black Sections proposal for constitutional recognition could no longer be brought year after year to Party Conference: if it was defeated in 1990 it was highly likely that the campaign would not get another opportunity until 1995!

The Composite 8 was approved at the October 1990 Party conference and called on the NEC to:

(a) Recognise formally and support black members' right to organise together for effective participation and representation.
(b) Make provisions for the representation of black members at all levels of the Party.
(c) Adopt the working party's proposal on black members' organisation within the Party that were presented to the National Executive Committee on 26 July 1989, namely, the setting up of a single affiliated organisation for members of African, Caribbean and Asian descent with local and regional groups and direct representation on the National Executive Committee.[42]

Black representation had finally been granted constitutional recognition within the Party, but at what cost? As the dust settles, it is worth making several concluding observations.

Separating Reality from the Rhetoric

Whilst the campaign for Black Sections failed to gain acceptance in its original form, the movement did succeed in making an important impact on black political development in Britain. Of its stated aims and objectives, the campaign was most successful in placing the issue of black representation on the political agenda. In doing so it had a direct effect on the selection and election of black

candidates for local and parliamentary offices. Black Sections served
as a catalyst in raising the consciousness of the Labour Party, and
the public at large, to the need for black political participation and
representation.

The real success of the campaign, therefore, has undoubtedly
been its symbolic significance. The campaign for Black Sections was
an important sign that black people were no longer content with
being passive observers of the political process. Where the
movement failed was in its efforts to galvanise grassroots support
and to mobilise the black community. For all its rhetoric, the
movement was unable to campaign more broadly on issues outside
the Labour Party's internal structures. Aside from publishing policy
papers such as *The Black Agenda*, the movement failed to attract
significant participation from the wider black community in its
attempts to link into large-scale protests and demonstrations
around issues such as the Newham Seven, the Broadwater Farm
Defence Campaign, the Handsworth Defence in 1987 and the
injustices committed against individuals like Clinton McCurbin and
Trevor Monerville.[43]

In many ways, the movement outlived its effectiveness.
Successful in increasing black representation, it became a victim of
its own success. With the election of more black councillors and the
emergence of black MPs, the Labour Party was let off the hook. The
campaign could no longer complain that the 'black perspective' was
not being represented. More importantly, the political parties now
had the option of consulting with these black representatives as
official tribunes of the black communities. In this respect, the
campaign was in a much weaker position after 1987.

The impact of the Black Sections campaign was also limited by
the character of the movement's approach, its style and tactics. Its
alliance with Labour's left, though in many ways inevitable,
ensured that it too would be a target for attack both by the media
and the Party leadership in its effort to put its electoral house in
order. In any case, if Women's Sections and Youth Sections were
any indication, then the influence that any sections could have had
was grossly over-estimated. Arguably, the Women's and Youth
Sections have had little effect on the recruitment and
representation of its members; rather, they have created small
enclaves in which ambitious members conduct sectarian battles

among themselves for the few extra delegated positions. Lord David Pitt, referred to by many as the 'elder black statesman', expressed his reservation early on about the ability of Black Sections to 'deliver' to the black community:

> My attitude about Black Sections has always been the same. You see, it is in an ironic situation. Black Sections are essentially damn good for the Labour Party, who do not want it, and of no use to black people, who seem to want it. It's good for Labour because it gets new members and increases black dependence and loyalty. But it will do nothing for blacks, just as sections have done nothing to help women. There is no real power in Black Sections.[44]

The decline of the Black Sections movement was further hastened by the internal strife created by the acrimony which developed between many of its leading members. The apparent shift of some of the black MPs, and their explicit disapproval of its tactics, marked a further decline for the campaign. The survival of the newly-formed affiliated Black Socialist Society will rely heavily on the ability of black activists to mend these internal divisions.

As an example of black self-organisation, the Black Sections movement has several important implications for future black political development. The obstacles the movement encountered in gaining black support, on the one hand, and party political acceptance on the other, imply that a solely 'race-specific' movement in Britain will never be wholly successful. The strength of any black movement rests ultimately on its legitimacy within the local black communities. Community activism will be crucially important in the 1990s given the current state of retrenchment among the main political parties. As 'mainstream' politics moves away from addressing black concerns, and a new bipartisan consensus is formed to keep 'race' out of electoral politics, it will become imperative for black communities to ensure that their interests do not drop off the agenda.

Notes

1. The *Guardian*, 5 October 1990.
2. Interview with Ben Bousquet, 26 February 1988.

3. Interview with Marc Wadsworth, 12 March 1988.

4. Interview with Diane Abbott, 25 February 1988.

5. Interview with Linda Bellos, 14 March 1988.

6. Interview with Phil Sealy, 10 March 1988.

7. Motion 28, Labour Party Conference, 1983.

8. Quoted in *The Times*, 12 December 1985 and 24 September 1985.

9. Quoted in Tony Sewell, 'The Last All-White Parliament', *New Statesman*, 1 January 1986.

10. Roy Hattersley at Labour Party Conference, 1985. See C. Rowley, 'The Campaign for Black Sections in the Labour Party', unpublished thesis, University of Warwick, 1986.

11. *New Statesman*, op. cit.

12. From the Report of the Labour Party Conference, 1985, cited in Rowley, *op cit.*

13. K. Shukra, 'Black Sections in the Labour Party', in Harry Goulbourne (ed.), *Black Politics in Britain*, Avebury, Aldershot 1990, p.173.

14. Interview with Andrew Carnegie, 25 February 1988.

15. Quoted in P. Webster, 'Kinnock Firm on Black Sections', *The Times*, 24 May 1985.

16. There were 2 composite resolutions in the 1985 conference favouring Black Sections. One was defeated 5,350,000 votes to 1,169,000, while the other was rejected by a vote of 5,982,000 votes to 538,000. Interestingly, the motion opposing Black Sections was narrowly defeated 3,383,000 to 3,091,000.

17. Narendra Makenji, in 'This week, Next Week', 1988.

18. Tony Sewell, 'Black Sections: Only One Slice of the Cake', *The Voice*, 25 May 1985.

19. Harris Research Centre, *Political Attitudes Survey*, June 1987.

20. Interview with Paul Boateng, 25 May 1988.

21. Interview with Diane Abbott, *op.cit.*

22. Diane Abbott at Labour Party Conference, 1984. See also Rowley, *op cit.*

23. Bill Morris, in 'This Week, Next Week', 1988.

24. Quoted in David Upshal, 'Which Way Forward for Black Politics', *New Society*, 4 March 1988.

25. 'Black Representation in the Labour Party', *Race Today*, September/October 1984, p.3.

26. Quoted in David Upshal, *op.cit.*

27. *Ibid.*

28. Interview with Linda Bellos, 14 March 1988.

29. Interview with Russell Profitt, 11 February 1988.

30. Dr Tariq Modood, 'Who's Defining Who?', *New Society*, 4 March 1988.

31. Interview with Keith Vaz, 22 December 1987.

32. 'Four Sign with Kinnock', *African Times*, 24-30 April 1987. Sharon Atkin as a prospective Labour parliamentary candidate for Nottingham East, had remarked at a Black Sections Conference, 'I don't give a damn about Neil Kinnock and the racist Labour Party'. She was, as a result, removed from fighting that seat and suspended from the Labour Party.

33. There was an effort on Abbott's part to speak but she was not acknowledged. None of the black MPs were key speakers for the motion.

34. David Upshal, 'The Labour Party: An Anti-Racist Dilemma', *New Socialist*, December 1987, pp.36-7.

35. *Ibid.*

36. Interview with Paul Boateng, *op.cit.*

37. *Ibid.*
38. Rita Austin, Robin Corbett and Marian FitzGerald, 'Minority Report from the Working Party on Positive Discrimination', Labour Party Document, 30 May 1985.
39. Bill Morris, 'Time for New Thinking in the Black Sections Debate', *Caribbean Times*, 22 January 1988.
40. *Caribbean Times*, 29 January 1988.
41. Interview with Mike Wongsam, 16 August 1990.
42. Composite 8, Labour Party Conference, 1990, moved by Irma Critchlow (Streatham CLP) and seconded by Edward Niles (Islington North CLP). Carried. 4 October 1990.
43. Shukra, *op.cit.*, p.184.
44. Interview with Lord Pitt, 30 June 1988.

6 The General Election of 1987

The 'race card' was appallingly played in my campaign. Race was made an issue in the general election of 1987, largely by the media. We were all seen as black candidates only – not just parliamentary candidates with views on a wide range of issues, seeking to represent the whole of our constituencies.

– Zerbanoo Gifford

The general election of 1987 will be remembered for many things. Mrs Thatcher made history by being the first Prime Minister this century to win three successive victories, returning the Conservatives with a 102 seat majority over the other political parties. Not since Lord Liverpool in the 1820s had a leader been able to garner as many election wins.[1] For the Labour Party, the 1987 election was a final lesson that ultimately policies, not just a glitzy campaign, win elections. Indeed, the emerging realisation was that Labour still had some 'listening' to do, if it was to have any hopes of wooing back the British electorate. The 1987 election was also a poignant moment for the (now defunct) Alliance parties which had to come to terms with the fact that the mould of the two-party system had not after all been broken. But for black Britons, the election represented the first time that people of African and Caribbean descent would serve in the House of Commons. (The three previously elected black MPs had been of Asian descent.) With the election of four black Members of Parliament, including the first black woman, the dream of black parliamentary representation had finally become a reality.

Prelude

For all the political parties, the stakes were high going into the election. At risk were the reputations and credibilities of all the political parties. This was especially true for the opposition parties. The Conservative Party had the advantage of serving for two previous terms and commanding a comfortable majority in both. But the Thatcherism project had much of its agenda yet to accomplish and re-election was extremely important to them.

The Alliance parties also had great expectations in the wake of the 1983 election. That general election had shown them to be a formidable challenger, securing more than a quarter of the popular vote, only two per cent less than Labour. However, the precarious position the Alliance found themselves in after 1983 was that without proportional representation their support did not translate into an equivalent number of parliamentary seats. Thus 25.4 per cent of the vote only gave them 23 seats in the 1983 election, whereas Labour's 27.6 per cent gave them 209 seats. Despite little hope of changing the 'first-past-the-post' British electoral system in the immediate future, the Alliance still entered the 1987 election optimistically, encouraged by the SDP win in the Greenwich by-election in February that year.

The Labour Party had the most to lose by a poor showing in the 1987 election. At stake for Labour was yet another electoral defeat and the embarrassment of further encroachment by the Alliance parties. The Labour Party desperately needed to recover from the electoral trough they found themselves in after 1983. In this election Labour had secured its lowest share of the vote since 1918 and was reduced to 209 MPs, its lowest postwar figure.[2] This was due in part to further slippage in its traditional working-class base: alarmingly, the 1983 election survey studies revealed that only 38 per cent of manual workers and 39 per cent of trade unionists had voted Labour.[3] Polls had also found a loss of confidence in Labour's ability to deliver on defence and the economy. Combined with the failure of the Foot leadership in 1983, this made Labour highly cognisant of the need to present a unified party with Neil Kinnock as a strong leader for the 1987 election. But the sombre reality was that it needed a swing of over 10 per cent, twice as high as had been achieved in any postwar general election, in order to gain a working parliamentary majority.[4]

From the outset, the prospects for the 1987 election were not good for Labour. To add to the Party's misfortune, it was becoming clear that Britain was experiencing social changes that would benefit the Conservative party to the detriment of Labour. Britain was becoming more affluent and middle-class under Thatcher, in spite of the deprivation in some areas. A MORI survey revealed that between 1979 and 1987 home ownership increased from 52 per cent to 66 per cent of the population, and share-ownership from 7 per cent to 19 per cent. Likewise, reports revealed that the proportion of council tenants had dropped from 45 per cent to 27 per cent, and trade union membership had fallen from 30 per cent to 22 per cent of the work force. As two leading political scientists noted:

> Britain was becoming increasingly a nation of owner-occupiers and shareholders, and decreasingly one of the propertyless and of council tenants, belonging to trade unions and working in nationalised industries.[5]

These social trends were the stuff of which Conservative voters were made. It was against this background that the general election of 1987 was fought. Given its weakness, the Labour Party appeared the most vulnerable. It was in this context that 'race' made its appearance.

Race and the 1987 Campaign

After the 1983 election, the notion of 'ethnic marginal constituencies' and the myth of the 'black vote' were largely destroyed. The CRC report after the October 1974 general election had encouraged all the political parties to make efforts toward wooing the black electorate. In 1983, blacks were specifically targeted by the political parties, and initiatives were aimed at capturing the 'black vote' away from Labour. The Conservatives' 'Labour says he's black; Tories say he's British' advertising campaign and the Alliance's 'Sevenpoint Policy Package for the Ethnic Communities' were explicit appeals to black voters. Such overtly targeted efforts, however, had little effect. The 1983 results showed the black electorate to be the only (identified) group of

Labour voters to remain loyal. A Gallup poll after the election revealed that only 21 per cent of black Labour supporters defected, compared with 31 per cent overall.[6] Labour still garnered the majority of the black vote, securing 64 per cent compared with 21 per cent for the Conservatives and 15 per cent for the Alliance. No longer could it be said, however, that the other parties had written off the black vote without any consideration. In fact, the opposite was the case: the 1983 experience was followed by a backlash in which it seemed that more could be gained by targeting those alienated by a strong anti-racist stance than by pursuing black electors.[7]

Another reason why the black vote was not courted in the 1987 campaign has been attributed to what one political commentator has labelled the 'inhibiting effects' of the 1985 riots in Handsworth and Tottenham.[8] The aftermath of these riots, in which lives were lost, made the political parties reluctant to court black people. The political response in 1985 differed from the response to the riots of 1981 in which every effort was made to deflate the racial dimension. The riots in 1981 were described as an 'urban' problem, not as a 'racial' problem, and the public was pacified by the Government's assurance that such civil disturbances would be prevented in the future. After the violence in 1985, the mood of the country had changed and the evenhandedness of the Scarman Report was not repeated.

In 1987, 'race as a problem' did not surface, as it had done before, in the explicit form of populist polemics about immigration, crime and public order, but the 'race card' was played nevertheless in coded form.[9] The race factor was subsumed into the general context of a moral panic about 'extremism' associated with the Labour left which was a dominant theme in the election campaign, particularly in London. 'Race' was inscribed in the use of phrases like 'loony left' and the 'London effect'. These terms were popularised by the media who created controversy by giving a somewhat partisan account of the supposed extremism of some Labour controlled authorities (who had taken up the mantle of the former GLC's pioneering anti-discrimination policies).

Past experience had shown that when race was made an election issue, it was Labour which most often lost and the parties of the right that benefited. The Conservatives unexpected victory in the general election of 1970 was in part due to the appeal of Enoch Powell's infamous 'rivers of blood' speech. One academic estimated that the effect of the race factor gave the Conservatives a 2.5 per cent swing, while another suggested the swing was as high as 6.7 per cent.[10] Moreover, surveys showed that after Mrs Thatcher's notorious 'swamping' remark regarding immigration control, in January 1978, the Tories rose five points in the opinion polls.[11]

The Conservatives were not the only ones to benefit. The Alliance parties also successfully exploited Labour's vulnerabilities. In May 1986, the Liberals won control of the local authority in Tower Hamlets by one seat over Labour by allegedly appealing to the white racist vote.[12] Just four months before the 1987 general election, the SDP also won a dramatic victory over Labour during the February 1987 Greenwich by-election, turning a 1,211 Labour majority into a SDP majority of 6,611, and securing 53 per cent of the vote over Labour's 33.8 per cent.[13] While there was no overt campaigning on race, this loss was largely attributed to the 'London effect' – the supposedly negative effects of the active equal opportunity policies of some Labour left councils in the London area.[14] After the by-election, one leading Labour figure acknowledged the connection between Labour extremism and the race equality policies pursued by certain London Labour authorities, and cited it as detrimental among older voters.[15] Public attitude surveys showed a substantial increase in the proportion of voters agreeing that Labour was 'too extreme' from 53 per cent in January 1987 to 67 per cent in April 1987.[16]

The real irony, then, was that there was no overt appeal to racist sentiment, at least on a national level. Such an appeal not unknown in the past could have potentially backfired and damaged the overall credibility of the party who used it. More importantly, there was no reason to do so. The desired effect could be obtained as easily from exploiting the meanings and images which adhered to the notion of the 'loony left'.

The Loony Left: Labour Extremism and the Media

According to the majority of the press coverage this was clearly going to be Mrs Thatcher's election. She had received the endorsement of seven out of eleven national daily newspapers.[17]

Only the *The Guardian* and the *Daily Mirror* publicly supported or identified with Labour. Interestingly, while the Conservatives were picked as the favourites, Labour received most attention from the press. The *Sun*, for example, spent three column inches discrediting the Labour Party for every inch in defence of the Conservatives' policies. In the tabloid papers, the overall ratio for coverage of Conservative, Labour and Alliance was 5:6:3. With the exception of the *Daily Telegraph*, which was distinctly anti-Labour, the quality daily newspapers were more balanced in their coverage. The ratio of coverage for the Conservatives, Labour and Alliance was 5:5:4.[18]

For the tabloid papers, Labour extremism, with its emphasis on gay rights, anti-sexism and anti-racism was the recurring theme. The repertoire of classic sensationalism, amounting to an orchestrated propaganda campaign, included such headlines as:

MILITANT BLACKS HOLD GUN TO LABOUR!
  – *Daily Mail*, 16 March 1987
LABOUR ROW AS KINNOCK SACKS BLACK MILITANT
  – *The Times*, 30 April 1987
WHERE THE HARD LEFT IS POISED TO STRIKE
  – *Daily Mail*, 7 March 1987

The Labour-controlled Brent Council came under special fire in the McGoldrick case. Maureen McGoldrick, headmistress at Sudbury School in Brent, was suspended by the authority pending an inquiry into allegations that she had made racist remarks. The *Daily Mail*, in an article entitled, 'Gay Rights and Race ... the Key Issues in the Row', trumpeted McGoldrick as 'the most celebrated victim of a loony left council policy'.[19] The article went on to denounce another London 'leftie' council, Lambeth, for allegedly establishing 'a lesbian and gay working party which condemned Neighbourhood Watch schemes as a way of spying on homosexuals'. The final attack in the article was made against the 'hard left' Hackney authority. The *Daily Mail* reported: 'Hackney in East London, spent 15,000 on its 'Lesbian Strength and Gay Pride' Festival in June and provided 100,000 to counter discrimination against homosexuals among town hall employees'.

Several personalities were singled out as the 'looniest' of the loony left. Most notably featured were Black Sections activists and

Labour's black parliamentary candidates, who were closely identified with the hard left. Frequently, they were referred to as the 'militant' Diane Abbott or the 'radical' Paul Boateng. None was as maliciously labelled as Bernie Grant. Former leader of the 'left-wing' Haringey council, Grant had been quoted as saying the police 'got a bloody good hiding' during the 1985 riot in Broadwater Farm in which a policeman was hacked to death. His remark was seen as publicly condoning the actions of the rioters and made him a ready target for the right. Ex-GLC leader Ken Livingstone and Bernie Grant appeared in the press more often than any other Labour politicians except Kinnock, Hattersley and Healey.[20] The personal antagonism directed against black candidates, Grant said, 'was nothing short of a witch hunt':

> The media hype was appalling. They would stop at nothing to destroy our credibility. We all got it but it was especially bad for me. I was seen as the biggest bogey person and so was Ken Livingstone. Our results, I think reflected this negative press. The problem was that we were not just local figures, we were national figures. So there was no need to play the race card locally, it was well played before – the whole time leading up to the election – thanks to the media.[21]

The irony was that it was difficult to claim that the attacks were racist, since the charge made against them was ostensibly because of their political views not their colour. Extremism was the crime, while public persecution and humiliation was the punishment.

A parody was made of their personal and political lives in order to undermine their credibility. No paper did it better than the *Sun*, at the time the bestselling daily paper in Britain. The *Sun* took extremism to the extreme. It was 'basic, bigoted and brilliant', commented one political observer:

> Basic because its main theme was the incompetence of the Labour Party – its Marxist ideology, its loony lefties, its fantasy defence policy, its windbag leader and its indebtedness to robber baron union bosses. Bigoted because *The Sun* not only made hay with any scandal it could find about Labour politicians, but also linked the party as a whole with sexual minorities ... Brilliant because this was all presented with a verve which no other paper could match.[22]

Only the *Sun* could have the audacity to dream up 'THE BLACK MANIFESTO: BAN ON LINKS WITH WHITES'. On 1 May, just days before the announcement of the election, the *Sun* proclaimed the intentions of Labour's 'black extremists' by enumerating their 'ten-point plan'. Included were such items as: (1) open up civil service and town hall jobs to blacks by lowering entry standard; (2) name national monuments and beauty spots after African revolutionaries; (3) open the floodgates to mass immigration by scrapping controls; and (4) forge links with Communist Cuba and other anti-American socialist states. Although it is questionable how much impact such imbecility had, it built up a picture of the Labour Party dominated by black militants and gay rights activists, and fundamentally unfit to govern.

The other political parties were quick to follow the lead of the popular press. During the election campaign both the Conservatives and the Alliance predicted that Labour's parliamentary contingent would be dominated by extremists. On 26 May, the Alliance revealed the names of '101 Damnations' – actual or potential Labour MPs with 'hard left' credentials. The Conservatives based their overall campaign attack against Labour on three main weaknesses: defence, the loony left and economic competence, devoting the whole of their second election broadcast to the theme of Labour extremism. The programme featured 'quotations from a familiar rogue's gallery headed by Bernie Grant and Ken Livingstone ... followed by clips of the excesses of 'loony left' councils, some of the more sinister-sounding parts of the Labour manifesto, and even the Alliance's list of 101 hard-left Labour candidates'.[23] The broadcast ended with the caption, 'HELP THE CONSERVATIVES STOP THE LEFT!'.

Labour Strikes Back

The Labour Party was well aware of the unpopularity of its left wing and the likelihood of that vulnerability being exploited. The Party had painfully learned the electoral liability involved when, in the early 1980s, it had moved further to the left. The election of Michael Foot over Denis Healey, and the breakaway and formation of the SDP by some of its most senior members, were among the more visible signs of its leftward tendencies, both of which cost the Party dearly in the 1983 election. Upon Kinnock's election to the leadership, efforts were made to improve this image.

Kinnock, who had himself been identified with the left of the

Party during his rise to power, quickly tried to distance himself and the Party from the negative 'public relations' effects of the hard left. The new leadership was especially concerned to present a united front and was determined to tackle its internal divisions.

One of the first targets in this process of change was the Militant Tendency. In a speech at the 1985 Party Conference, Kinnock made a powerful move by condemning the actions of the Militants in Liverpool. He denounced the 'grotesque chaos of a Labour council – a *Labour* council – hiring taxis to travel around the city handing out redundancy notices to its own workers'.[24] It was a controversial stance and not favoured by some members of the NEC, most notably Liverpool MP, the late Eric Heffer. The Militants came under siege again in 1986 when the Party conference voted to expel eleven leading Militant members, including Derek Hatton, after an NEC inquiry decided they had broken party rules. There is no doubt that Kinnock won respect from almost all quarters for his tough stance on the Militant Tendency.

The leadership's patience with its left-wing London authorities was also wearing thin, especially in the aftermath of the Greenwich by-election in which a safe Labour seat was lost to the Alliance. The Party's fears had been exposed when a letter from Patricia Hewitt, Kinnock's press secretary, was leaked to the press. In the letter Hewitt expressed grave concern over the 'London effect' and attributed to it the electoral backlash Labour was experiencing. Hewitt revealed:

> It's obvious from our polling, as well as from the doorstep, that the London effect is now very noticeable. The loony Labour left is taking its toll; the gays and lesbians issue is costing us dear amongst the pensioners; and fear of extremism [...] Private and public polling is now showing very clearly that whereas London at the height of the GLC campaign was pulling Labour's national average support up – London today is pulling Labour down.[25]

The publicity given to these alleged incidents of Labour authority 'excesses' was mounting: apart from the negative press coverage of the McGoldrick case in Brent, only weeks before the 1987 election, the Labour council in Islington came under fire. The SDP alleged that a white pupil in an Islington nursery school had been reprimanded for singing the nursery rhyme 'Baa Baa Black Sheep',

which council policy allegedly held to be racist.[26] Much effort was
made by Labour to contain the effects of this type of publicity, in
the hope of recovering by the general election. The image of the
Party's black activists proved to be no help in this process.

The Black Sections movement had become yet another thorn in
the side of Labour's progress. In late April 1987, the third Black
Sections National Conference was scheduled in Birmingham. In an
effort to forestall further abuse from hostile sections of the media,
Labour's deputy leader Roy Hattersley, ostensibly on behalf of all
the Birmingham Labour MPs, publicly expressed his opposition to
the meeting being held in his constituency and specifically warned
the black candidates to stay away. Most heeded the caution. Sharon
Atkin, parliamentary candidate for Nottingham East, did not. At the
conference, Atkin called the Party 'racist' and declared:

> I'm not a conformist, I'm a rebel [...] I was told not to come to this
> meeting tonight if I wanted my parliamentary seat. Well, I don't want a
> parliamentary seat if I can't represent black people. What I will always
> do is fight for black people [...] So I don't give a damn about Neil
> Kinnock and the racist Labour Party.[27]

Sharon Atkin's combative stance (unfortunately for her) afforded
the Labour leadership an opportunity for retribution. The NEC
decided by a 19-6 vote that Atkin's remarks entailed a serious
breach of the Party's constitution, and she was suspended.
Although the Nottingham East constituency still supported her
candidacy, the iron fist of the Labour leadership struck again and
mandated that she be replaced by a political moderate, Mohammed
Aslam. The point was well made: the activities of Labour's more
strident members would no longer be tolerated. Thus strong
support for black autonomy became part of the Party's definition of
'extremism'. Black activists had become part of the 'enemy within'
of Labour. Although the association of the hard left with the Black
Sections movement was partly to blame for this demonisation, the
Labour leadership must be criticised for its inability to distinguish
between tendencies within black politics, and its collusion with the
'loony left' discourse, of which racism was clearly a powerful
component. If support for racial equality was perceived as an
electoral liability, it would be sacrificed.

Unlike 1979 and 1983, when there was direct competition for the black vote and black candidates were a novelty to be nurtured, in 1987 it was evident that black candidates were no longer 'people in glass houses', where 'none dared throw stones'.[28] After the Atkin affair, many of the black candidates appeared to fall in line. As mentioned earlier, four leading black candidates (Abbott, Boateng, Grant and Profitt) made a statement distancing themselves from Atkin. They felt it necessary to restate their loyalty:

> We want to place on the record that as parliamentary candidates we are accountable to constituency Labour parties and that we will be fighting the general election on the manifesto drawn up on the basis of Party policy. There can be no other position.[29]

Some black activists and members of the hard left were appalled and infuriated by the Party leadership's action in the Atkin case and by what they viewed as the subsequent 'cowardice' of the four black candidates. *Labour Briefing*, a journal on the hard left of the Party, denounced the 'witch hunt' tactics of the Labour leadership and responded:

> In just six weeks, the leadership has alienated trade unionists, black people, peace campaigners, and lesbians and gays. All in a frantic bid to be more patriotic than the Tories and more moderate than the Alliance.[30]

There was an element of truth in this caricature: Atkin had in effect become an unfortunate sacrificial lamb on the altar of a potential Labour victory.

Black Candidates

This was the political climate that set the tone for the black candidacies in the 1987 election, but the emergence of black parliamentary candidates must be seen as part of an evolutionary process. After an absence for more than fifty years of black parliamentary representation, black candidates followed a steady, but hard won progression from unwinnable, to marginal, and finally to safe seats.

In the immediate postwar years there were very few black candidates for the major political parties. The first postwar black candidate for one of the major parties was Sardar K.S.N. Ahluwala, who stood for the Liberals in Willesden West in 1950. He received only 2,853 votes, just over 5 per cent of the total votes cast in the constituency.[31] The most prominent black parliamentary candidate was Dr David Pitt (presently Lord Pitt), who first stood in 1959 for Labour in Hampstead, a seat that Labour had no chance of winning. Pitt polled 13,500 votes, 28.3 per cent of the total votes cast in Hampstead. He lost on a 3.5 per cent swing against him, compared with a national swing of 2.6 per cent against Labour overall.[32] There were no black candidates standing on behalf of the main political parties during the 1964 election, although there was one independent. However, in 1970 David Pitt stood again, along with three Liberals and three independents.

The 1970 candidacy of David Pitt, this time in Clapham, a fairly safe seat, was a major setback for black political representation. The results are now infamous in the annals of black electoral representation in Britain. Pitt was dramatically defeated on a 10.2 per cent swing from Labour to the Conservatives, double the swing in neighbouring constituencies. Compared with the national loss of 4.9 per cent, the Labour Party's vote in Clapham was down 11.2 per cent and the total turnout had decreased by 11 per cent. The total Labour vote was down by 6,082 votes from the 1966 election, from 19,555 to 13,473 in 1970. The Tories gained the seat with a majority of 3,120.[33] The inference was unavoidable: David Pitt had lost votes because of the colour of his skin. 'I don't delude myself, I know race was an issue', Lord Pitt acknowleged. 'But I still insist that if I had three months instead of three weeks to prepare for the election I would not have done so badly [...] I believe if they got to know me, they would have taken a different point of view. It's too easy to blame things solely on race.'[34] Nevertheless, it is hard to deny the conclusion that was drawn from his 1970 defeat that party loyalties were volatile when fielding black candidates. The legacy of Pitt's demise was to haunt the candidacy of blacks for years to come.

It was not, in fact, until the general election of 1979 that more than two black candidates stood for one of the main political parties.[35] In that election there were five principal black parliamentary candidates – two Conservatives, two Liberals and one Labour. The 1979 election also marked the first time in postwar history that the Tories selected a black candidate. But even so, this presence was largely tokenistic, since none of them stood a real chance of winning.

Thus, in the years before 1983, black candidacies had been few and far between, largely in unwinnable seats, and perceived as vulnerable to the 'race factor'. However by 1983 the number of black parliamentary candidates had risen to eighteen. All of the major parties were fielding black candidates – six Labour and four each for the Conservatives, Liberals and SDP. There were also seven independent black candidates.[36] Paul Boateng, contesting Hertfordshire West for Labour, was the only candidate that stood a chance – becoming the first black candidate since David Pitt to contest a marginally winnable seat.[37] However Boateng not only lost the former Hemel Hempstead seat that Labour had won in 1979, but finished a poor third behind the SDP candidate. Labour received only 22.3 per cent of the vote, while the Conservatives won 46.7 per cent and SDP 31 per cent. Boateng lost on a two-party swing of 18.3 per cent.[38]

Although Boateng had suffered a similar fate to Pitt in statistical terms, his defeat was mainly due to circumstances other than 'race'. There was a bitter dispute within the local CLP about the selection of Boateng over the former MP, Robin Corbett, which divided Labour supporters. This, along with his close association with the GLC and 'hard left bogeyman', Ken Livingstone, were the cause of much adverse publicity. The combination greatly reduced the likelihood of Boateng winning, regardless of his ethnic origin. Although it was easy to interpret his result as further proof of the electoral liability of black candidates, Boateng's results were not in line with the other black candidates in 1983.

There was, in fact, no significant difference in the performance of most black candidates than the results of any other candidate from their respective parties. In seventeen of the eighteen constituencies with black candidates, where comparison with the result in 1979 was possible, the parties' position remained the same in 1983.[39] Post-election analyses found that the effects of voter discrimination or prejudice were negligible and suggested that the party, not the candidate, was the determining factor.[40] It was argued upon these results after the 1979 and 1983 elections that if blacks were now to be selected for 'safe' seats, they would be as likely to win as any other candidate. Had the ghost of David Pitt's 1970 failure finally been laid to rest? The general election of 1987 was the real test.

The Politics of Selection

For the 1987 election, 27 black candidates were selected to stand
for the major political parties. It represented an increase of nine
from the 1983 general election and included six Conservatives,
fourteen Labour, six SDP and one Liberal. 1987 was most
significant because of the number of blacks chosen to fight safe and
marginally winnable seats. For Labour, the six parliamentary
hopefuls included Paul Boateng (Brent South), Diane Abbott
(Hackney North/Stoke Newington) and Bernie Grant (Tottenham)
in safe Labour seats; and fighting in marginals were Russell Profitt
(Lewisham East), Keith Vaz (Leicester East) and Sharon Atkin
(Nottingham East) who was replaced by Mohammad Aslam. The
Tories also claimed to have two black candidates who stood a slight
chance of winning: John Taylor was chosen for Birmingham Perry
Barr and need a 7.3 per cent swing to take the seat from Labour;
more promising was Nirj Deva selected to stand for Hammersmith,
which only needed a 3.1 per cent swing.

Several factors precipitated the selection of black candidates and,
in turn, black representation more generally. The riots of the 1980s
served as a catalyst to black political participation in Britain.
However unwelcome, the riots of 1981 and 1985 did raise the
awareness of the nation to the needs and demands of black people.
Diane Abbott specifically attributed her election to this effect:

> The riots posed a serious threat to the whole community relations-race
> relations industry, by exposing it as a failure. So they had to face the
> truth. They were forced to address black involvement and black
> political participation. I, along with other black candidates, directly
> benefited from this.[41]

Similarly, the campaign for Black Sections in the Labour Party has
also been cited by many black candidates as a contributory factor to
their selection, both indirectly and directly. The best known
example of Black Sections activity was the selection of Russell
Profitt in Lewisham East. As a result of the involvement of Black
Sections, his candidacy was nullified by the NEC as were those of
the four other candidates selected through Black Sections
involvement. Profitt, however, unlike the other four Black Sections
candidates, was reselected by his constituency party, in opposition

to the NEC ruling, and his candidature was allowed to stand. He asserted:

> Unlike previous campaigns to have black representation, Black Sections provided a well-organised group of people involved at a grassroots level [...] Lewisham East was the first place where this tactic was successfully used to bring about the selection of someone who was black. I saw my selection very much as part of that campaign.[42]

While it is difficult to know the extent to which black under-representation was considered by selectors, in some constituencies which chose black candidates, the impact was clearly evident. This appears to have been a major consideration in the selection of Paul Boateng in Brent South, for example. 'It was very natural to choose a black candidate' confirmed one member of the Brent South Labour Party. 'There was a general acceptance that Brent South should be represented by someone who truly reflected the multi-racial nature of the community.'[43]

While selectors' attitudes can sometimes benefit black hopefuls, precedent suggests that the attitudes of selectors are more often biased *against* choosing a black candidate. The overwhelming tendency is to select white, middle-class candidates – more often than not educated, professional men.[44] A survey of the 1983 parliamentary winners showed that only 11.6 per cent were women and of all the new MPs less than 15 per cent did not have further education, while less than five per cent came from a background of manual employment.[45] Manifestly this composition works to the disadvantage of black people who are disproportionately working class. While the Labour Party was traditionally less conventional in this respect, even Labour's own make up has become increasingly less working class. In 1983, two-thirds of all Labour MPs came from non-manual occupations and over half were university educated.[46] In 1987, the proportion of Labour MPs who were manual workers was 29 per cent, the lowest since 1974.[47]

However the most pernicious factor working against the selection of black candidates remains the popular perception that black candidates lose votes, even though, as has been noted, this perception has been contested by several commentators (see note 38). For example, a study by John Bochel and David Denver on the selection process in the Labour Party discovered that black

candidates were considered to be an electoral liability by selectors.
The study found that 23 per cent of white selectors thought that a
black candidate would be a great disadvantage; 48 per cent thought
they would be some disadvantage; 25 per cent thought it would
make no difference and only 2 per cent believed it would actually
be some advantage. Interestingly, 51 per cent revealed that they
would be in favour of the Party taking positive action and selecting
more black candidates; while 9 per cent of those not in favour of
positive action said they would support a black candidate in a
constituency with a large black electorate but not otherwise.[48] The
results of this study are not surprising. The reality is that black
candidates seeking support for their nomination are greatly
dependent on white support, but there no guarantees that even
black selectors will prefer a black candidate.

The mandatory reselection rule of the Labour Party was a
decisive factor in the selection and subsequent election of two black
candidates in 1987. Only six sitting Labour MPs were directly
ousted by the reselection process, two of whom were replaced by
black Prospective Parliamentary Candidates. The deselection of
Norman Atkinson (Tottenham) and Ernie Roberts (Hackney North
and Stoke Newington) and the selection of Bernie Grant and Diane
Abbott in those respective constituencies were important
developments. Unlike the other four deselected, both Atkinson and
Roberts were ideologically on the left of the Labour Party: both
deselections were bitter, hostile battles. In Tottenham, Atkinson
and Grant were both local personalities; the former having served
as MP for Tottenham since 1964, and the latter as leader of
Haringey Council. Roberts in Hackney was at a disadvantage
because of his age (74), but even so received many more
nominations than Abbott. Nevertheless, he was defeated on a 42-35
vote by the former press officer for Lambeth. Abbott explained:

> Hackney has one of the largest black populations in London and there
> was enormous pressure from the black community outside the Labour
> Party to select a black candidate this time. I replaced the sitting MP and
> it was a very unpleasant and acrimonious process. He very much
> resented being displaced, particularly by a black woman.[49]

The success of Abbott and Grant suggest that the reselection
process could be an effective yet unpopular way for black activists

to get winnable seats. It is a means by which traditional incumbents, none of whom were black before 1987, can be forced to make way for those representing a new approach to the political arena. But it also means that the black MPs are subject to the same scrutiny and the possibility of deselection.

The growing importance of prior political experience has been increasingly a factor in the selection process, and this has enabled black activists to work their way through to selection, so that local involvement can pave the way to the national scene. Local government has become a recruiting ground for future MPs. In 1983, nearly 50 per cent of MPs elected had served as local councillors, and the overall proportion from political backgrounds increases considerably if the number of ex-trade union officials, political advisors, and other full-time party workers are also included.[50] In 1987, the Labour Party in particular had a disproportionate number of MPs and candidates being drawn from the ranks of local government officers, full-time politicians and trade union officials.[51] At least half of Labour's 14 black candidates in 1987 had a background in local government, most as councillors. Moreover, of all the black candidates in 1987 across the parties, nearly half had identifiable prior political experience. On the one hand this means that there is available to black councillors a route through to selection. On the other hand it means that black candidates are likely to be drawn from a fairly small pool. Keith Vaz specifically attributed his selection to political maturity more than any other factor:

> I think it's lack of political experience – lack of membership of a political party – that is the greatest handicap for black people [...] It is that length of service that is very important. And those who say that it was the advent of the Black Sections movement that caused black politicians and black MPs to be selected and elected miss the point.[52]

The implication of Vaz's statement is that black activists, like other party members, must pay their dues and climb the political ladder, demonstrating their loyalty and merit as others have done.

This attitude is especially prevalent among the black Tory candidates, many of whom see the growth in the number of black candidates selected for their party as part of a natural progression, as black members gain more political experience in the

Conservative Party. John Taylor, the first Afro-Caribbean Conservative parliamentary candidate in history when he fought Birmingham, Perry Barr, felt that his candidacy was only the beginning and that more black Tory candidates would be seen in the future:

> It was a great thing to have blacks fighting safe Labour seats, but that was also more predictable, more foreseeable. But the real test will be to have a black Conservative candidate fighting a safe Tory seat and winning. And that day of reckoning is coming.[53]

It is ironic the Mr Taylor himself subsequently would be the one to test his Party's commitment, as he was chosen to fight the Tory seat of Cheltenham in the 1992 election amid much controversy. Unfortunately, although he received strong backing from the Conservative Central Campaign Office, the local electors of Cheltenham proved to be unwilling to elect a black MP. Taylor's confidence implied a belief in a smooth and even progress towards enhanced black political representation. The real state of affairs was not so straightforward, as was indicated by his defeat. While the selection of six black candidates in 1987 for safe and marginal seats suggested that the ghost of David Pitt had been laid to rest, a look at some of the local campaigns of black parliamentary candidates might leave one wondering whether the spirit of Peter Griffiths at Smethwick had not been resurrected.

Campaign '87

While it is not within the scope of this study to comment on the individual campaigns of all the black candidates, this section does, however, seek to provide an overall feel for the kinds of campaigns that were waged and the varying tactics employed. What becomes apparent is that the 'race card' was being played locally against many of the black candidates, especially against Labour candidates.

It must be noted at the outset that the extent to which local campaigns actually affect the outcome of elections is unquantifiable. In fact, it has been suggested that local campaign activities have very little effect on electoral outcomes which are strongly influenced by national trends. Black candidates are subjected to the same ebb and flow of electoral fortunes as all candidates. Moreover, evidence suggests that electors have usually made up their mind by the time the election is called, so even national campaigns often only serve to reinforce prior decisions (see Table 6.1).[54]

As documented earlier in this chapter, race was made a factor in the campaign, but in more coded form and this was reflected in the local campaigns as well. Their opponents had to do little more than play upon the popular perceptions and images already projected in the national media.

Table 6.1

'When Did You Make Up Your Mind How You Would Vote Today?'

	Total	White	Asian	West Indian	Other
Base	4589	4371	63	53	36
Today	8%	7%	6%	11%	17%
During the last week	10%	10%	20%	13%	14%
Since election was called	21%	21%	27%	15%	28%
Some time before	60%	60%	41%	60%	42%
Not sure	1%	1%	2%	–	–

Source: Harris Research Centre, Exit Poll, 11 June 1987.

'Of course, the race card was played against me', Russell Profitt, Labour candidate for Lewisham East declared. 'That shouldn't be surprising; the Tories have always sought any advantage they could'.[55] Ben Bousquet, Labour candidate for Kensington, acted shrewdly: 'They expected me to play up the fact that I am black first and to make a big deal about it. When I didn't, they were shocked. You see, they expect black candidates to "wear our race on our sleeves"; we cannot afford to fall into that trap.'[56]

Not all the opposition to black candidates was from without. Diane Abbott, who replaced the sitting Labour MP Ernie Roberts for Hackney North, encountered much antagonism from Roberts' supporters, many of whom refused to campaign on her behalf. The Alliance candidate, Zerbanoo Gifford, standing for the Liberals in Harrow East, suffered a similar experience:

> I received no help from my local Party. No help at all. The selection was a bitter battle but I won narrowly. Many in the Party were so adamantly opposed to me that they went to neighbouring constituencies to canvas before they would help me.[57]

Bernie Grant, Labour candidate in Tottenham, also fell prey to a divided CLP, caused mainly by the ousting of sitting MP, Norman Atkinson.

The lack of support and organisation within the Party, in most instances, was offset by the participation of black supporters in the campaign itself. The experience of most black candidates suggests that black people, many for the first time, enthusiastically participated in canvassing on their behalf. 'It was exciting to see the number of black people who came out to help me. For the first time, I think black people felt they had a real stake in the election', Diane Abbott maintained.[58] Likewise, Gifford revealed that 'the support I received from the Asian community was what got me through. There was great warmth among my people who were excited and proud that I was standing'.[59] Keith Vaz also acknowledged the significance of this enthusiasm:

> The support I received from the Asian and black community was phenomenal. The election campaign we ran here was very similar to the election campaigns in America. We could actually say in black areas, 'Vote for Keith Vaz'.[60]

Interestingly, once again, the two black Tory candidates made a point of stressing the fact that the race card was not played against them, unlike most of the other black candidates. As in the selection process, Taylor insisted:

> Race was not an issue in my campaign. It was very difficult to play the race card against me because I was the only black candidate who didn't seem to be talking about colour. I was simply the Conservative candidate and that is the way my opponents dealt with me. We attacked each other on policies not personalities.[61]

Nirj Deva, in Hammersmith, asserted:

> I must have spoken – canvassed – close to 8,000 to 9,000 people during the campaign and I only heard of two people who said they wouldn't vote for me because I was an Asian. Two out of close to 10,000.[62]

The prejudice they admitted encountering was among blacks who took exception to them because they were black *Conservatives*. Both Taylor and Deva made the distinction that it was among

Afro-Caribbeans, not Asians, that this attitude was most prevalent. Taylor commented on the black backlash he experienced on the doorstep during his campaign:

> If I had any prejudice, I honestly think it might have been among the West Indians because they felt like – 'I'm not going to vote for an Uncle Tom' [...] Among the Asians there was a different reaction. I found that they were more prepared to listen to me. And for some I could see there was a measure of support there. It was much harder to break through the barriers with West Indians because they have such strong perceptions about the Conservative Party. They think you are a Tory, so you're against sanctions for South Africa [...] I have to say that it was the younger West Indians not the older ones that gave me the most difficulty. The older West Indians are more traditionalist and could see what I was about. The younger ones couldn't.[63]

The implication, as the 1987 results showed, was that party loyalty for blacks was stronger than ethnic identification. Black people won't vote for black candidates just because they are black.

While most black candidates could cite a few examples of explicitly racist attacks during their campaign, Zerbanoo Gifford's experience in Harrow East, appears to have been by far the worst:

> I came up against racism all the time. It was a very nasty campaign, very dirty. My campaign helpers and I were verbally abused – and spat upon on the High Street. Many refused to canvas because people were so rude to them – calling them 'nigger lover'. They couldn't believe it. I was so abused: Death threats, windows broken and car smashed up. It was just appalling![64]

The abuse against Gifford was also documented in the press, though often condescendingly. The *Mail on Sunday*, in an article entitled 'My Nightmare of Race Terror', depicted Gifford as a 'very attractive housewife' who had become the victim of 'a vicious sustained campaign of racial terror'.[65] Although hers was a particularly repugnant experience, most of the black candidates interviewed felt to varying degrees that race had been made an issue locally and nationally, in such a way as to place an obstacle in the way of their electoral success.

The Results: How Black Candidates Fared

Despite some instances like Zerbanoo Gifford, the results in 1987 confirmed the findings in 1983 that black candidates are not necessarily electoral liabilities. Although race does play a role in voter choice, factors other than race have a greater impact on election results. In most constituencies party loyalty takes precedent over individual preferences. Only in a very few marginals is there enough discrepancy that voter discrimination would adversely affect the outcome. Michel LeLohé made this political observation in an analysis of the general election of 1983. By constructing 'model' constituencies, LeLohé compared the results of black candidates with those of whites in similar constituencies. He discovered that there was evidence of voter discrimination in the 1983 election but that the average amount came to only 3 per cent. LeLohé then concluded that there were only 30 seats where this loss of votes would be enough for a black candidate to lose a seat. 'The corollary', he suggested, 'is that they would not lose any of the others'.[66]

Above all, the 1987 contest was historic in that it witnessed the election of four black MPs. Their victory put to rest the mythology that black candidates could not win elections. Moreover, the election of Keith Vaz – perhaps the biggest triumph – suggested that black candidates have the capacity to turn even marginals into winnable seats. The success of the four black MPs did not come, however, without some cost. As Table 6.2 reveals, many of the black candidates suffered swings greater than the national average against them, while only seven experienced experienced swings in their favour. Crucially, however, the size of the swing was not significant enough to make a difference between victory and defeat for any of the candidates.

Among the political parties, the Alliance candidates fared the worst. All seven did worse than expected; on average their vote fell by 7.7 per cent. An interesting comparison with the Alliance candidates of 1983 can be made. In five of the eight constituencies which had a black Alliance candidate in 1983 but a white one in 1987, the Alliance vote rose this time. For all eight constituencies the average change was −0.4 per cent, a swing away from the Alliance lower than the national average.[67]

The Conservative black candidates suffered a similar fate to the Alliance candidates. Only John Taylor received a swing in the Party's favour (0.4 per cent). Nirj Deva in Hammersmith was the Tory's main hopeful, becoming the first black Conservative to stand

Table 6.2

General Election of 1987
How Black Candidates Fared

Candidate – Constituency Swing

Conservative

R. Chandran	Preston	4.5 to Lab
N. Deva	Hammersmith	4.5 to Lab
N. Khan	Birmingham Spark	1.6 to Lab
K. Nath	M Blackley	4.1 to Lab
P. Nischall	Birmingham	1.5 to Lab
J. Taylor	Birmingham	0.4 to Con

Labour

D. Abbott*	Hackney	1.8 to Con
V. Anand	Folkestone	0.5 to Con
M. Aslam	Nottingham	1.5 to Lab
P. Boateng*	Brent S	3.4 to Con
B. Bousquet	Kensington	1.1 to Lab
B. Grant*	Tottenham	6.8 to Con
N. Hafeez	Stafford	1.2 to Con
A. Patel	Eastbourne	0.5 to Lab
P. Patel	Brent	0.9 to Con
R. Profitt	Lewisham	3.2 to Con
C. St Hill	Mid-Staffs	1.9 to Lab
M. Savani	Sheff Hallamm	2.5 to Lab
K. Vaz*	Leicester E	2.8 to Lab
V. Vaz	Twickenham	0.3 to Con

SDP

M. Ali	Blackburn	4.8 to Lab
B. Chahal	Liverpool R'side	5.5 to Lab
S. Fernando	Nottingham	7.0 to Lab
L. Kamal	Wakefield	6.7 to Lab
M. Moghal	Bradford W	13.8 to Lab
G. Sangha	Birmingham Lady'd	8.9 to Lab

Liberal

Z. Gifford	Harrow E	5.0 to Con

* Elected

Source: Guardian, 19 June 1987

in a marginally winnable seat. Deva did increase his Party's share of the vote by 2.6 per cent, but Labour squeezed the centre vote much more successfully to take the seat with a 4.5 per cent swing.[68]

Ironically, the party that encountered the most hostility for being

Table 6.3

Regional Swings for Black Candidates in 1987

	Difference from Projected Party Swing
Seats fought by 5 black Tory candidates	−2.54
Seats fought by 14 black Labour candidates	−1.94
Seats fought by 7 black Alliance candidates	−5.23

Source: British Public Opinion, MORI, August 1987

'soft' on race, performed the best overall. *Table 6.3* shows that Labour's black candidates performed more in line with their projected swing than either the Tory or Alliance candidates. The further irony is that while the other political parties exploited Labour's image on race in 1987, they suffered something of an 'own goal' when it came to the final outcome.[69]

Undoubtedly, however, the campaign against Labour extremism waged in the media took its toll on the black Labour candidates, especially in London. Among the main Labour hopefuls, all suffered swings against them with the exception of Keith Vaz, who stood outside London. (However, a number of exceptional factors had contributed to reduce the Leicester East Labour vote in 1983, so that the swing was calculated from an atypical base line.) Russell Profitt in the marginal seat of Lewisham East lost with a 3.2 per cent swing to the Conservatives.

Table 6.4

General Election 1987
Results of the Four Black MPs Compared with 1983

	1987	1983
Brent South	Electorate 61,020 Total Vote 40,724	Electorate 62,783 Total Vote 39,912
Paul Boateng	Lab 21,140 (51.9%) Con 13,209 (32.4%) Lib 6,375 (15.7%)	Lab 21,259 (53.3%) Con 10,740 (26.9%) Lib 7,557 (18.9%)
	Maj 7,931	Maj 10,519

4.41% Lib to Con
Turnout 64.87%   Turnout 63.6%

Hackney North/ Stoke Newington	Electorate 66,771 Total Vote 38,817	Electorate 66,754 Total Vote 36,493
Diane Abbott	Lab 18,912 (48.7%) Con 11,234 (28.9%) SDP 7,446 (19.2%) Green 716 (2.6%)	Lab 18,989 (52.0%) Con 10,444 (28.6%) Lib 7,746 (15.7%) Others (3.6%)
	Lab Maj 7,678 Swing 1.82% Lab to Con Turnout 58.13%	Lab Maj 8,545 Turnout 54.7%
Tottenham	Electorate 76,092 Total Vote 50,271	Electorate 67,944 Total Vote 43,092
Bernie Grant	Lab 21,921 (43.6%) Con 17,780 (35.4%) Lib 8,983 (17.9%) Green 744 (1.5%) Gait.Lab 638 (1.3%) WRP 205 (0.4%)	Lab 22,423 (52%) Con 13,027 (30.2%) Lib 6,990 (16.2%) Ind 652 (1.5%)
	Lab Maj 4,141 Swing 6.78% Lab to Con Turnout 66.06%	Lab Maj 9,396 Turnout 63.4%
Leicester East	Electorate 66,372 Total Vote 52,159	Electorate 67,071 Total Vote 49,092
Keith Vaz	Lab 24,074 (46.2%) Con 22,150 (42.5%) SDP 5,935 (11.4%)	Lab 18,184 (37%) *Con 19,117 (38.9%) SDP 10,362 (21.1%)
	Lab Maj 1,924 Swing 9.42% SDP to Lab *Lab GAIN from Con Turnout 78.58%	Con Maj 933 (1.9%) Turnout 73.2%

Abbott, Boateng and Grant were elected but on a decreased share of the votes by 3.3 per cent, 1.4 per cent and 8.4 per cent respectively (see Table 6.4). On the other hand, the 'London effect' was by no means restricted to Labour's black candidates: while Boateng suffered a 1.4 per cent decline in Labour's vote, Ken Livingstone – dubbed 'Red Ken' by the press – in the neighbouring constituency of Brent East won narrowly, with the percentage if the Labour vote declining by 4.4 per cent. Similarly, Diane Abbott's results (down 3.3 per cent) was exactly in line with those in the next door Bow and Poplar constituency, where the candidate Mildred Gordon was also labelled as extremist but did not gain nearly as much attention.[70]

The Labour result that stood out the most was that of Bernie Grant in Tottenham. Grant suffered the largest swing against Labour of any of their black candidates with a 6.8 per cent swing to the Conservatives. In comparison to neighbouring constituencies, he polled about 10 per cent less than he should have.[71] Bearing in mind the usual caution that must applied to survey data, Harris Research Centre conducted an interesting poll in Tottenham the week before the 1987 election which offers hints as to why Grant performed so poorly.

The survey suggested that electors in Tottenham considered Bernie Grant's personality, actual or perceived, to be as significant as party allegiance in making their decision. Grant was undoubtedly affected by the hostile press coverage he received surrounding his comment during the Broadwater Farm incident. A further Harris survey showed the impact of the media campaign against him: within his constituency, 42 per cent of the respondents agreed that Grant held extreme views on issues like law and order, while only 24 per cent disagreed. Irrespective of race and voting intention, more people believed that Grant was extreme than didn't.

Table 6.5

Tottenham Poll
Do Bernie Grant's Personal Characteristics
Affect the Likelihood of Voting for Him?

| | | Voting Intentions | | | Race | |
	Total	Con	Lab	All	White	Non-White
Base	587	110	278	369	210	
More Likely	22%	2%	40%	8%	15%	34%
Makes No Difference	32%	22%	36%	27%	41%	
Less Likely	32%	66%	14%	55%	13%	
Don't know/Not stated	14%	10%	10%	10%	13%	

Source: Harris Research Centre, 4 June 1987

Undeniably, the best performance for a black candidate in 1987 was Keith Vaz in Leicester East. Vaz turned a Conservative majority of 933 in 1983 into a Labour majority of 1,924 in 1987, receiving 46.2 per cent of the vote to the Conservatives' 42.5 per cent. Vaz attributed his success chiefly to the large turnout among ethnic minority voters: 'the turnout in the predominantly black wards was almost 95-96 per cent. You could go down into the heart of the Asian community during the election and almost every single house had a Labour poster on it [...] without the high turnout in the black vote, I doubt we would have won.'[72] Vaz's anecdotal impression seems to be borne out by the electoral statistics. While the Tory vote in Leicester East did increase from 1983 by 3.6 per cent, the overall turnout also increased from 73.2 per cent in 1983 to 78.58 per cent in 1979, well above the national average. Although the proportional increase in the black vote is unknown, it is highly likely that it would have made up a significant part. Other candidates endorse this sensation of a groundswell of black support. Paul Boateng maintained, 'my campaign sparked the interest of many blacks who were first time voters because they believed the system finally had something to offer them'.[73] The extent to which this interest translated into a higher turnout of black voters is less obvious outside Keith Vaz's constituency: the turnout in Hackney North rose 3 per cent on 1983, but Brent South only slightly over 1 per cent.

While the real impact of black support for black candidates is unknown, what is clear is that black voters do not support black candidates just because they are black. Rather the black electorate, like the white, vote along party lines, as the results for independent black candidates dramatically illustrate. What appears more plausible is that black people may be more likely to vote for someone who is of their own colour *and* of their own party, as opposed to someone who is simply of their own party. What ever the case, the black electorate in the 1987 election remained overwhelmingly loyal to Labour. The Harris political attitudes survey of non-white voters revealed that 72 per cent of all ethnic minorities intended to vote Labour in the 1987 election, compared with only 18 per cent for the Conservatives, and 10 per cent for the Alliance (see table 6.6).[74] Afro-Caribbeans remained the most faithful, with 86 per cent expressing their intention to vote Labour, while 67 per cent of Asians continued to pledge their support.

Table 6.6

Voting Intention of Blacks in General Election 1987

	Total	Ethnic Group Asian	Afro-Caribbean	Ethnic Concentration High	Low
Base	820	592	228	709	111
Con	18%	23%	6%	15%	39%
Lab	72%	67%	86%	77%	43%
Lib/SDP Alliance	10%	10%	7%	8%	17%
Don't know/ Other	–	–	–	–	1%

Source: Harris Research Centre, Political Attitudes Survey of Non-White Voters, 25–29 May 1987

Similarly, another Harris survey showed that the majority of black people in all social classes still vote for the Labour Party (Table 6.7).

Table 6.7

Black Party Support by Class, 1987

	A,B	C1	C2	D,E
Base	48	206	241	290
Conservative	33%	30%	14%	10%
Labour	54%	52%	78%	84%
Alliance	13%	17%	9%	5%

Source: Harris Research Centre, 25-29 May 1987

Conclusion

The fear of a white working-class backlash continues to loom over any advance the Labour Party might make towards the black electorate. The slight leakage in Labour support observed among black people in 1987 stands in stark contrast to the haemorrhage in the Party's support among the white working class. The most salient feature of the Conservatives' victory in 1987 was its consolidated strength among working-class voters. The Tories received 40 per cent of the C2 voters (skilled working class), compared with Labour's 36 per cent; and 54 per cent among the upper middle class (ABC1) voters, compared with Labour's 18 per cent.[75] The comprehensive Conservative victory in 1987, as in 1979 and 1983, was largely built on support from what Ivor Crewe has called the 'New Working Class' - skilled workers who live in the south, who are home owners, who are employed in the private sector, and who are not members of unions.[76] A MORI post-election poll showed the Conservatives receiving 44 per cent of the vote among working-class voters who were owner-occupiers, while Labour received only 32 per cent. In contrast, black working-class voters continued to be faithful: 52 per cent of C1 voters intended to vote Labour, compared with 30 per cent for the Tories; and 78 per cent of C2s supported Labour, while only 14 per cent preferred the Conservatives.

Labour emerged from the general election of 1987 once again struggling to maintain its white working-class support in the South, rather than its black support. This made it very apparent which group the Party would be more likely to target in the next general election. With the evidence from the 1987 election suggesting that a mass defection from the Labour Party by its black supporters was highly unlikely and most definitely not imminent, the days of 'courtship' with the black electorate have long gone. None of the political parties have much incentive to recruit the black vote. For the Tories and the Liberal Democrats the 1987 results reinforced the widely held perception that black people would remain faithful, if they voted, to the Labour Party. Likewise for Labour, the election of its first black MPs removed the pressure of black representation and by most accounts satisfied at least for the time being its liberal obligations. While the black community during the general election of 1987 scented the sweet smell of parliamentary victory, this has turned a little sour with the current prospect that more votes may be had by playing the race card than courting the black vote.

Notes

1. Election commentary from David Butler and Denis Kavanagh (eds), *The British General Election of 1987*, Macmillan, London 1988.
2. *Ibid.*, p.47.
3. Marian FitzGerald, *Black People and Party Politics*, Runnymede Trust, London 1987, p.51 (hereinafter *op cit*).
4. *Ibid.*
5. Butler and Kavanagh (eds), *op.cit.*, p.4. There is some speculation that these figures may be slightly over-estimated.
6. FitzGerald, *op.cit.*, p.51.
7. Marian FitzGerald, *Political Parties and Black People*, Runnymede Trust, London 1984, p.13.
8. Marian FitzGerald, 'Black Sheep: Race in the 1987 Campaign', Unpublished Paper, October 1987, p.1 (hereinafter 'Black Sheep').
9. *Ibid.*
10. W. Miller in *British Journal of Political Science*, Vol.10, No.1, 1980, and D. Studlar in *American Political Science Review*, No.72, 1978.
11. Mary Ann Sieghart, 'A Deep Division but a Pointless Row', *New Statesman*, 24 April 1987.
12. *New Statesman*, 15 May 1986. The Liberal-controlled authority of Tower Hamlets dismantled the former Labour administration's race committee and received much publicity for its eviction of homeless Bangladeshi families. See also FitzGerald, 'The emergence of Black Councillors and MPs in Britain'.
13. Butler and Kavanagh (eds), *op.cit.*, pp.312-3, and FitzGerald, *op.cit.*, 'Black Sheep', p.12.
14. Austin Mitchell, 'Today', BBC Radio 4, 7 March 1987.
15. Patricia Hewitt, formerly Neil Kinnock's press secretary, quoted in *Daily Mail*, 7 March 1987.
16. Butler and Kavanagh (eds), *op.cit.*, p.68.
17. Martin Harrop, 'Press' in Butler and Kavanagh (eds), *op.cit.*, p.163.
18. *Ibid.*
19. *Daily Mail*, 7 March 1987.
20. Harrop, *op.cit.*, p.171.
21. Interview with Bernie Grant, June 1988.
22. Harrop, *op.cit.*, pp.168-9.
23. Martin Harrison, 'Broadcasting' in Butler and Kavanagh (eds), *op.cit.*, p.156.
24. Butler and Kavanagh, *op cit.* p.52.
25. *Daily Mail*, 7 March 1987.
26. FitzGerald, 'Black Sheep', p.52.
27. *Asian Times*, 8-14 May 1987.
28. FitzGerald, *op.cit.*, 1987, p.47.

29. *Asian Times*, 29 April-5 May 1987; see also *African Times*, 24-30 April 1987.

30. Quoted in *Asian Times*, *op cit*.

31. Muhammad Anwar, *Race and Politics*, Tavistock Publications, London 1986, p.98.

32. *Ibid*.

33. *Ibid*., p.99.

34. Interview with Lord David Pitt, June 1988.

35. In the February 1974 general election, Bashir Mann stood in East Fife for the Labour Party. Mann won 6,634 votes, just 15 per cent of the total. The Liberals also fielded Dhani Prem in Coventry South East, where he received 11.7 per cent of the vote (4,472). In the October 1974, Cecil Williams stood for the Liberals in Birmingham Sparkbrook, winning 2,921 votes (9.8 per cent).

36. None of the seven independent black candidates received more than 970 votes, and their worst result was only 54 votes. The 1983 election also marked the first time that the number of black candidates standing for the main political parties (18) outnumbered the independents (7).

37. Russell Profitt had been selected in the safe Labour seat of Battersea North, but in the constituency merger with Battersea South because of boundary changes, he lost out to the sitting MP, Alf Dubs.

38. Butler and Kavanagh (eds), *The British General Election of 1983*, Macmillan, London 1984, p.314.

39. Anwar, *op.cit*., p.106.

40. FitzGerald, 'Are Blacks an Electoral Liability?', *New Society*, 8 December 1983; see also Michel Le Lohe, 'Voter Discrimination Against Asian and Black Candidates in the 1983 General Election', *New Community*, No.11, Autumn/Winter 1983.

41. Interview with Diane Abbott, 25 February 1988.

42. Interview with Russell Profitt, 11 February 1988.

43. Interview with Jonathan Hall, June 1987.

44. See for example, Colin Mellors, *The British Members of Parliament: A Socio-Economic Study of the House of Commons*, Saxon House, Farnborough, 1978.

45. FitzGerald, *Political Parties and Black People*, p.89-90.

46. FitzGerald, *op.cit*., 1984, p.90.

47. Butler and Kavanagh (eds), *op.cit*., p.20.

48. John Bochel and David Denver, 'Candidate Selection in the Labour Party', *British Journal of Political Science*, Vol.13, January 1983, pp.45-60. See also FitzGerald, *Political Parties and Black People*, p.91.

49. Interview with Diane Abbott, *op.cit*.

50. FitzGerald, *op.cit*., 1984, p.90.

51. Byron Criddle, 'Candidates' in Butler and Kavanagh (eds), *op.cit*., p.193.

52. Interview with Keith Vaz, 22 December 1987.

53. Interview with John Taylor, 6 February 1988.

54. Butler and Kavanagh (eds), *op.cit*., p.241.

55. Interview with Russell Profitt, *op.cit*.

56. Interview with Ben Bousquet, 26 February 1988.

57. Interview with Zerbanoo Gifford, 30 January 1988.

58. Interview with Diane Abbott, *op.cit*.

59. Interview with Zerbanoo Gifford, *op.cit*.

60. Interview with Keith Vaz, *op.cit*.

61. Interview with John Taylor, *op.cit*.

62. Interview with Nirj Deva, *op.cit.*

63. Interview with John Taylor, *op.cit.*

64. Interview with Zerbanoo Gifford, *op.cit.*

65. *Mail on Sunday*, 6 April 1988.

66. Michel Le Lohé, 'Voter Discrimination Against Asian and Black Candidates in the General Election', *New Community*, Vol II, Autumn/Winter 1983, p.107-8. See also FitzGerald, *New Society*, 8 December 1983, p.396.

67. Butler and Kavanagh (eds), *op.cit.*, p.341.

68. *Ibid.*

69. FitzGerald, 'The emergence of Black Councillors and MPs', *op.cit.*

70. FitzGerald, 'Black Sheep', p.8.

71. Butler and Kavanagh (eds), *op.cit.*, pp.341-2.

72. Interview with Keith Vaz, *op.cit.*

73. Interview with Paul Boateng, *op.cit.*

74. The survey's sample involved interviewing 1,007 black people: specifically, 871 black people were questioned in 40 sampling points in areas of high black population; a further 136 black people, all but three of whom were of Asian descent, were interviewed by telephone in areas of low black population, including Dorking, Edinburgh and Ipswich.

75. Butler and Kavanagh (eds), *op.cit.*, p.275.

76. Ivor Crewe, *The Guardian*, 15 June 1987; see also Butler and Kavanagh (eds), *op.cit.*, pp.275-6.

7 'New Realism' in the 1990s

> Our election marked an advance. The gains made by blacks in British politics can be very transitory. We cannot afford to take anything for granted. To talk about watersheds and floodgates opening would be premature. In terms of the future, we must see this recent progress as a window of opportunity. Whether black people stay in the frame or disappear depends on our performance in particular, the black community and outside circumstances.[1]
>
> – Paul Boateng, MP

This book began by describing the 'new activism' of the 1980s on the part of both the British polity and black Britons. It was over this period that a variety of favourable circumstances combined to enable the most significant advances to date in black political representation. From the 1981 riots in Brixton and Toxteth to the campaign for Black Sections within the Labour Party, black people made great strides towards gaining an effective political voice. Likewise, the political parties themselves appeared to be much more responsive to black demands.

Encouraged by reports of the potential importance of the 'black vote', all the major political parties gave visible signs of courting the black electorate in the general elections of 1979 and 1983. From campaign literature and party manifestos to the recommendations of the Scarman Report, the British political establishment gave indications of a heightened awareness of their responsibility for the problems caused by racial discrimination. Equally, black activists in the 1980s were prepared to test the sincerity of these gestures by placing unyielding pressure on them to deliver the goods. It was the combination of these factors which created an atmosphere conducive to the increase in black political participation that

154

culminated in the election of the four black MPs.

While a time of great exultation, their election campaign also brought signs of a changing political wind. The decade that began with a 'new activism' ended with a 'new realism'. The sobering state of affairs that has emerged at the beginning of the 1990s is that the main political parties are now, at best, coolly neutral on issues of 'race'. Certainly the Labour leadership, still nervous of any repetition of 'the London effect', is unlikely either to countenance any new phase of black militancy or to produce its own anti-racist initiatives. Having finally settled the rumbling issue of Black Sections by the institution of the Black Socialist Society, Labour will venture nothing that might have an adverse effect on their electoral respectability. The Tories, on the other hand, have shown a marginal shift away from the Thatcherite hostility towards the 'race relations industry'. But while the 'classless society' envisaged by John Major, and the selection of John Taylor, suggest a new, mildly anti-racist, egalitarian tone from Central Office, it is extremely doubtful whether this public relations exercise will ever translate, for example, into tougher anti-discrimination legislation.

At the same time, while the door has been closing on progress and reform, black Britons have been unable to keep their own house in order. During the 1980s the internal strife, though present, was generally subordinated to the immediate objective of securing a voice in the decision-making process. The growth in black local and parliamentary representation which resulted, however, has proved not to be the cure-all. While black representation serves an important symbolic and lobbying function, it is by no means the sole solution to black political emancipation. Disillusioned by their relative powerlessness, the fragile and perhaps illusory unity that did exist around securing a political voice quickly dissipated. The biggest challenge facing ethnic minorities in Britain is to build unity and cohesion in the midst of obvious difference and discordance. Instead of seeking a single unitary black identity, perhaps it is more realistic that unity can be achieved around issue-specific concerns – those shared common problems that affect all people of colour. Never has the need been so great than during the present period of retrenchment.

The most obvious sign of stagnation in the sphere of formal politics has been in the selection of black parliamentary candidates.

In contrast to the increase in the 1980s which witnessed a rise from six in 1979 to 27 black candidates fighting parliamentary seats for all three main parties in 1987, in the 1992 election there were only 23 ethnic minority candidates – 10 for Labour, 8 for the Conservatives and 5 for the Liberal Democrats. In addition, a number of black Labour candidates saw their local selection procedure frozen for up to a year due to membership problems. These included Nottingham East, Bethnal Green and Birmingham Perry Barr and Small Heath.[2]

Of the eight Tory candidates, two were standing in Conservative-held seats, Nirj Deva who moved from Hammersmith to Brentford and Isleworth, and John Taylor, who – amid great acrimony between (white) local Party members – was chosen for the relatively safe Conservative seat of Cheltenham (see Chapter 3). Taylor's selection and subsequent defeat gives rise to speculation as to whether the Tories will ever again 'experiment' with black candidates in white constituencies for fear of inciting a racist backlash.

Interestingly the Conservative record in 1992 was an improvement on 1987, when there were only six black candidates, none of whom were standing in Conservative-held seats. However, the number of ethnic minority candidates selected by both the Liberal Democrats and Labour dropped – the Liberals from 7 (Alliance) to 5, and Labour from 14 to 10.

Perhaps most depressing has been the passing-over of black parliamentary candidates by the Labour Party, and the NEC interference in the local selection process. Three poignant examples remain fresh in the memory, and in each case a black candidate was overlooked and a white one selected. Ben Bousquet, who twice stood as the Labour parliamentary candidate for Kensington in both 1983 and 1987 and who had increased the Labour vote against national and regional trends, was deselected during the 1988 Kensington by-election, losing to Ann Holmes, a white professional woman, on a close 21-23 vote. While some commentators point to the internal politics of the local CLP as the reason for his demise, others suggest the presence of an unwillingness to field a black candidate. Bousquet commented: 'I was warned that they would take the seat away from me as soon as I made it winnable for them and they did.'[3]

The treatment of black candidates in the Vauxhall by-election in 1989 provides a high-profile example which reflects the Labour leadership's intense nervousness about standing black candidates in

safe or marginally winnable constituencies, even in a seat like
Vauxhall that has a sizable black population and includes the
heartland of Brixton. The NEC imposition of Kate Hoey in
Vauxhall, a Labour stronghold, even over a thoroughly credible
black candidate such as Russell Profitt (three-time Labour
parliamentary candidate), exemplified the extent of the Walworth
Road headquarter's control. For many black activists the
interference was inexcusable. Similarly in 1990, Labour failed to
reselect Chris St Hill, the 1987 candidate, to fight the
Mid-Staffordshire by-election but instead chose Sylvia Heal who
won the marginal seat on the back of a surge of anti-Tory sentiment.
(She lost the seat in 1992.) The subliminal, if not overt, message is
that black candidates are electoral liabilities and that the political
parties can no longer accept the risk.

Future black representation is further complicated on a local
level by the restrictions imposed under the 1988 Local
Government Act which prohibits elected members in one local
authority from holding senior political posts in another. This
regulation will have a disproportionate effect on the recruitment of
black councillors since black activists are more often employed by
local government. The local race, education and housing units
(especially in inner-city boroughs) provide a natural seed-bed for
black politicians, providing invaluable experience in government
and administration as a preparation for political office. The direct
impact of this legislation on the selection of black councillors has
not been studied, but the May 1990 local elections did witness a
decline in the number of black people standing and saw the defeat
of several high profile black councillors.

The Future of Black Political Development in Britain

The greatest political achievement of black Britons during the
1980s was the increased participation of black activists in
community, governmental and electoral politics. But the harsh fact
is that having black political representatives does not eradicate
racial discrimination nor its effects. The daily plight of the majority
of black Britons remains largely unchanged. What the presence of
black councillors and MPs has done is provide an *avenue* for blacks

to lobby the mainstream, but their ability to bring about change in black communities is limited by partisan and bureaucratic considerations.

So while the election of four black MPs was an historic achievement, its real significance has largely been symbolic. The black MPs have been limited in the influence they can exercise by the fact that three of the four are backbenchers in the Opposition, although Paul Boateng has been promoted to the Labour frontbench as a shadow spokesman for the Treasury. Keith Vaz acknowledges the constraints they face: 'We have to be realistic about how much four black people can really do to change the lot of all blacks, our hands are tied by the same bureaucracy that impedes others.'[4]

Black Britons, therefore, have obtained little direct political power by having black MPs. Ironically, Bernie Grant, as leader of Haringey, had a greater source of influence and authority than he currently exercises as an MP. His situation highlights the disparity between obtaining status and achieving political power:

> In terms of real power, I gave that up when I stepped down as leader of the council. Then I was in control of a budget and the decision-making apparatus. I realise the much greater limitations of being in Parliament, but our election takes on a different type of importance. Here we have a higher platform from which to voice the concerns of black people.[5]

This problem of powerlessness is not just unique to black activists in the Labour Party, the same is equally true for the other political parties. The advancements of black Tories such as Baroness Shreela Flather to the House of Lords, are important contributions but at a symbolic rather than executive level.

The impact of such symbolic gains cannot be measured in tangible terms but one should not underestimate the difference the presence of black elected officials has made in the 'collective unconscious' of the British public. For *The Times* even to suggest the 'Affable Reality of Not Being Barmy Bernie', in a favourable profile of Bernie Grant, is a sign of a gradual bending in popular perception.[6]

At the same time, however, these few high-profile black

representatives are forced to shoulder a burden of expectation and responsibility on the part of their black constituents and supporters which simply does not apply to their white counterparts. Especially as they gain a degree of acceptance in the mainstream of formal politics, they become prey to accusations of 'selling out', co-option and careerism, from the more critical elements in black communities.

Given the limitations and problems of black electoral representation, mainstream participation can only be half of the dual strategy for black political development in the 1990s. As it becomes more difficult to manoeuvre in the mainstream, it will become more important to turn inwards to political mobilisation within black communities. The challenge is to win better educational and economic opportunities for black people that will provide benefits beyond the current retrenchment in electoral politics.

Community activism complements, builds and strengthens black representation – the majority of ethnic minorities conduct their affairs outside the orthodox political arena. Grassroots activism within black communities has been and continues to be the lifeblood of black political development. Community activists, most of whom are not members of political parties, working with specific local projects, have had the most direct impact on the day-to-day lives of black people. The challenge is to build on that community base and turn it into an effective political and electoral force.

Developing a Distinctly British Model of Black Political Empowerment

The second prong of the strategy for black political development in the 1990s is that this dual approach of placing pressure inside and outside the system must operate under a distinctly British model of black political empowerment. Too often, in both rhetoric and action, black British activists have looked to the black American experience of a 1960s-style mass unitary black movement as the quintessential model for black political struggle. While there are similarities and lessons to be learned, the fallacy would be to assume that the same strategies and tactics can be used in both cases. Black activists often exaggerate the extent to which blacks have achieved political power in the USA. Though significant advances were made in the 1960s, the reality is that by 1986 there were 6,424 black elected officials, and presently there are less then 8,000, which represents only one per cent of the total number of elected officials in the USA.[7] It is important not to overestimate the degree of power which black Americans have actually obtained.

Three main factors exclude the possibility of an American-style civil rights movement in Britain: first, the intensely tradition-bound culture of the British political system; second, the relatively small size of the population and modest level of black identification; and finally, the different mode and history of oppression in Britain from the African-American experience.

Progress for black Britons demands considerable political acumen. The British model for black political participation must take into account the relative weight of class in British politics. The class-based culture of British politics places a permanent restraint on black political development: this is the single most important lesson for black activists. National initiatives based *solely* on race will never wholly be accepted. The British polity cannot accept it and, more importantly, a substantial portion of black people do not want it. Increasingly they see themselves as black British, which has meant creating an identity in a society which is characterised strongly by its cultures of class.

Politics in the United States, in contrast, is based on a principle of pluralist competition between various ethnic, economic, religious and regional groups, as an integral part of 'the American way'. Governmental powers in the USA are highly decentralised, allowing for greater local political and economic independence. The emergence of black mayors in the large metropolitan cities, for example, means that black officials have relative autonomy to govern their own areas. In Britain, local government has become increasingly subordinate to central government, especially during the Thatcher administrations, with the abolition of regional metropolitan authorities and the policies of rate- and charge-capping. Experience has suggested that even if black people become leaders of councils – the British equivalent to American mayors – their ability to exert political power is greatly restricted by central government's monitoring and manipulation of the financial purse strings.

The black British model must also be tempered by the very obvious but unavoidable fact that black people comprise only 5 per cent of the population in Britain, while in the USA the black population is almost triple that figure, with more than 13 per cent. In both cases, black people are highly concentrated in the inner cities, but the implications are quite different. Whereas African-Americans have become the majority in such cities as Detroit, Atlanta, Philadelphia and Cleveland, even in the highest concentrations of black populations in (parliamentary) constituencies in Britain, the proportion barely reaches 50 per cent. In the USA, the sheer multiplicity of political offices and tiers of government (state, federal, district, municipal, county) ensures greater opportunity for politically active black Americans. The nature of black identity also differs enormously between the two countries: in Britain, there is no uniform black identity and efforts to create one have resulted in acrimony and failure; but almost all American blacks identify with an Afrocentric perspective. This important distinction made possible the building of a mass unitary movement in the American context.

It was, moreover, the legacy of legalised segregation promulgated through 'Jim Crow' laws that made a mass civil rights movement necessary. Generations of institutional and legally enforced racial discrimination necessitated affirmative action to provide blacks with an equal opportunity to compete. These tactics used in the USA are not directly translatable to the British black experience. Black Britons suffer from more subtle forms of discrimination, the more covert legacy of colonial subordination. Because Britain never experienced such overt and systematic segregation as the American South, the effects of institutional racism have often been conveniently hidden behind a policy of benign neglect.

Despite all these differences, lessons can be learned: Britons can look towards the USA for advances in social policy, especially with regard to equal employment opportunities. But black Americans also face their own specific dilemmas: the major gain of the civil rights movement was the development of a comfortable black middle class who still benefit in the present climate, but possibly to the exclusion of the masses of poor blacks. The irony, of course, is that African-Americans themselves are unable to reproduce another mass civil rights movement. The early successes of the 1960s movement have now produced sharp divisions of socio-economic status within the black community.

Yet in both countries, there are sources of strength that point to potential solutions. In the USA, there is a more identifiable black leadership and a greater pool of political resources (given the comparative educational and economic advantages of African-Americans) which will greatly enhance their ability to face the challenges of the 1990s. Conversely, the relative socio-economic homogeneity of Britain's black communities could prove to be a favourable condition for possible political alliances. The approaches may be different but the challenge in both countries is the same – how best to address race-specific concerns in a political culture and establishment that appears reluctant to heed their demands.

To meet this challenge, it is imperative that black Britons develop a formula for progress that is congruent with the changing political reality of Britain. Success will then depend on the degree to which black activists and the British polity are prepared to compromise. Significant gains were made in the 1980s, and it is important that these should be consolidated and built upon. Although the outlook for the 1990s is difficult, there are still possibilities for real change.

Notes

1. Interview with Paul Boateng, 28 May 1988.
2. C. Hynes, 'Labour Selection Move Sparks of New Fear', *The Voice*, 29 January 1991.
3. D. Upshal, 'Bousquet Bites the Bullet', *New Statesman*, 8 July 1988.
4. Interview with Keith Vaz, 22 December 1987.
5. Interview with Bernie Grant, 28 June 1988.
6. Mick Brown, 'The Affable Reality of Not Being Barmy Bernie', The Times, 3 July 1988.
7. Joint Centre for Political Studies (Washington DC, 1986). For further reference, see Chuck Stone, *Black Political Power in America* (New York, 1970); Michael Preston, *The New Black Politics* (New York, 1982); James Conyers and Walter Wallace, *Black Elected Officials* (New York, 1976).

Postscript: The 1992 General Election

There were 23 ethnic minority candidates for the main political parties in the 1992 General Election (see table 8.1). This represented a decrease from the 27 candidates who stood in 1987. As has been noted, the number of Conservative candidates increased from 6 to 8; however, the number of Labour candidates decreased from 14 to 10 and the Liberal Democrats decreased from 7 to 5.

The trend towards the return of the invisibility of race – in either selection, or as an electoral issue – continued. Perhaps this trend, which coincides with the Conservative philosophy on race, contributed to the Conservatives' improved performance. In addition, John Major's position is probably more fully in harmony with the official 'race blind' policy than was Margaret Thatcher's. However, it should be noted that only three of the Conservative candidates (Deva, Taylor and Popat) were standing in winnable or marginal seats.

The main focus of black hopes, and therefore disappointment, continues to be the Labour Party. It seems that in its bid to hold the centre ground, to 'go respectable', the Party has been prepared to lower its profile on race as an issue, and to make no effort to support black candidates. This was reflected in the decline in the number of black candidates, the failure to select a number of excellent candidates (see pp.156-7), and the absence of debate on issues of race during the election.

The number of black MPs has now increased to six, five of whom are Labour. The four black MPs elected in 1987 all retained their seats with increased majorities, with an average swing to Labour well above the national average. (This probably reflects, in part, a

Table 8.1.   Ethnic Minority Candidates in the 1992 General Election

Party	Candidate name	Constituency	Place	No of Votes	% 1992	loss or gain	% 1987
Lab	Diane Abbott*	Hackney N & Stoke N'ton	1	20,083	57.8	+9.1	48.7
Lab	Kingsley Abrams	Wimbledon	2	11,570	23.3	+1.7	21.6
Lab	Claude Ajith Moares	Harrow West	2	12,343	22.5	+5.3	17.5
Lab	Mohammed Akhbar Ali	Liverpool Riverside	1	2,498	9.2	-2.0	11.2
Lab	Paul Boateng*	Brent South	1	20,662	57.5	+5.6	51.9
Lab	Doreen Cameroon	Ashford kent	3	11,365	20.0	+5.3	14.7
Con	Lurline Champagnie	Islington North	2	8,958	23.7	-1.6	25.3
Con	Abdul Qayyum Chaudhary	B'ham Small Heath	2	8,686	25.0	+3.8	21.7
Con	Nirj Joseph Deva	Brentford & Isleworth	1	24,752	45.8	-1.9	47.7
Lib	Zerbanoo Gifford	Hertsmere	3	10,681	18.9	-4.9	23.8
Lab	Bernie Grant*	Tottenham	1	25,309	56.5	+12.9	43.6
Lab	Piara Khabra	Ealing Southall	1	23,476	47.4	-3.3	50.7
Con	Mohammed Khamisa	B'ham Sparkbrook	2	8,544	24.8	-0.9	25.7
Lab	Askhok Kumar*	Langbaugh	2	28,454	43.1	+4.7	38.4
Libdem	Pash Nadhra	Ealing Southall	4	3,790	7.7	-5.7	13.3
Con	Andrew Popat	Bradford South	2	20,283	38.4	-2.4	40.8
Con	Mohammed Riaz	Bradford North	2	15,756	32.2	-7.3	39.5
Con	Mohammed Rizvi	Edinburgh Leith	3	8,496	21.1	-1.8	22.9
Libdem	Vin Sharma	Halesowen & Stourbridge	3	7,941	12.4	-9.6	22.1
Con	John Taylor	Cheltenham	2	28,683	44.7	-5.4	50.2
Lab	Keith Vaz*	Leicester East	1	28,123	56.5	+10.4	46.2
Libdem	Marcello Verma	Cynon Valley	4	2,667	7.0	-5.2	12.2
Libdem	Peter Verma	Cardiff S & Penarth	3	3,707	7.8	-7.6	15.4

* sitting MP

Source: *Runnymede Bulletin*, May 1992

recuperation of votes lost when they initially stood.) Ashok Kumar, who won Langbaugh for Labour in a by-election in 1991, lost his seat, although he increased Labour's percentage of the vote. The new Labour MP, Piara Khabra, was elected in Ealing Southall, a constituency with an ethnic minority population of over 50 per cent.[1] There has long been pressure in this constituency for an Asian candidate. Thus the increase in the number of ethnic minority Labour MPs is as a result of a long overdue selection – which was resisted by Sid Bidwell who had held the seat for over twenty years.

The election of a black Conservative MP, Nirj Deva, representing Brentford and Isleworth, is very welcome. Deva has long been a prominent supporter of the Conservative Party, having previously contested Hammersmith and Fulham. He was standing in a seat with a sizeable ethnic minority population,[2] and inheriting an 8000 majority from Sir Barney Hayhoe, who retired after 18 years as MP. There was no controversy surrounding his selection, and his election shows that in the right kind of seat, it is possible for a black Conservative candidate to succeed.

Unfortunately, John Taylor's experience in Cheltenham showed that traditional Tory seats – prosperous white suburbs and rural Southern England – are not the 'right' kind of seats for black candidates. Taylor's election campaign was surrounded by controversy and marred by racist incidents, and a section of the local Conservative Party actively opposed his candidacy. Taylor was quoted by *The Voice* as saying, 'There is a small group working against me. I was told that they celebrated my defeat'.[3] Clearly it was for these reasons that Taylor was defeated. There was a swing away from the Conservatives of 5.2 per cent in Cheltenham, whereas for the country as a whole there was a swing from the Liberal Democrats to the Conservatives of 2.06 per cent. A Cheltenham businessman summed up the situation as follows: 'The selection committee were politically naïve to think that a coloured gentleman could hold the seat here'.[4]

While it is good news that the four black MPs elected in 1987 held their seats, and that two new black MPs have joined them in the House of Commons, it is unlikely that there will be further breakthroughs in the next period. Ironically, it is probably the Conservative Party, notwithstanding the Cheltenham fiasco, that will improve its performance in the immediate future.

Notes

1. According to Mohammed Anwar's estimates (see p.19), the 1987 figure for the ethnic minority population in Ealing was 55.6 per cent.
2. Anwar's estimates for the Brentford and Isleworth ethnic minority population in 1987 was 16.7 per cent.
3. Quoted in the *Runnymede Bulletin*, May 1992.
4. *Evening Standard*, 10 April 1992.

Bibliography

Books

Anwar, Muhammad, *Race and Politics*, Tavistock Publications, London 1986.

Anwar, Muhammad, *Voters and Policies: Ethnic Minorities and the General Election, 1979*, Commission for Racial Equality, London 1980.

Belott, Max and Gillian Peele, *The Government of the UK: Political Authority in a Changing Society*, Weidenfeld and Nicolson, London 1985.

Benyon, John (ed.), *Scarman and After*, Pergamon Press, London 1984.

Brown, Colin, *Black and White Britain: The Third PSI Survey*, Policy Studies Institute, London 1984.

Butler, David and Kavanagh, Dennis, *The General Election of 1983*, Macmillan Press, London 1984.

Butler, David and Denis Kavanagh, *The General Election of 1987*, Macmillan Press, London 1988.

Butler, David and Stokes, Donald, *Political Change in Britain*, Macmillan Press, London 1974.

Carter, Trevor, *Shattering Illusions: West Indians in British Politics*, Lawrence & Wishart, London 1986.

Centre for Contemporary Cultural Studies, *The Empire Strikes Back: Race and Racism in 1970s Britain*, Hutchinson, London 1982.

Cottle, Thomas J., *Black Testimony: The Voices of Britain's West Indians*, Wildwood House, London 1978.

Deakin, Nicholas (ed.), *Colour and the British Electorate 1964*, Pall Mall Press, London 1965.

Field, Simon, Muir, George, Rees, Tom and Stevens, Philip, *Ethnic Minorities in Britain: A Study of Trends in their Position Since 1961*, Home Office Research Studies Report No.68, London 1981.

FitzGerald, Marian, *Black People and Party Politics in Britain*, Runnymede Trust, London 1987.

FitzGerald, Marian, *Political Parties and Black People: Participation, Representation, and Exploitation*, Runnymede Trust, London 1984.

Fryer, Peter, *Staying Power: The History of Black People in Britain*, Pluto Press, London 1984.

Gilroy, Paul, *There Ain't No Black in the Union Jack*, Hutchinson, London 1987.

Goulbourne, Harry (ed.), *Black Politics in Britain*, Avebury, Aldershot 1990.

Heath, Anthony, Jowell, Roger and Curtice, John, *How Britain Votes*, Pergamon Press, Oxford 1985.

Jones, Bill and Kavanagh, Dennis, *British Politics Today*, Manchester University Press, Manchester 1983.

Layton-Henry, Zig, *The Politics of Race in Britain*, George Allen & Unwin, London 1984.

Layton-Henry, Zig (ed.), *Race, Government, and Politics in Britain*, Macmillan Press, London 1986.

Mellors, Colin, *The British Members of Parliament: A Socio-Economic Study of the House of Commons*, Saxon House, Farnborough 1978.

Milbrath, Lester W. and M.L. Goel, *Political Participation*, University Press of America, Washington DC, 1982.

Phizacklea, Annie and Miles, Robert, *Labour and Racism*, Routledge and Kegan Paul, London 1980.

Pulzer, Peter G.J., *Political Representation and Elections in Britain*, George Allen & Unwin, London 1975.

The Runnymede Trust and the Radical Statistics Race Group, *Britain's Black Population*, Heinemann Educational Books, London 1980.

Sarlvik, Bo and Crewe, Ivor, *Decade of Dealignment*, Cambridge University Press, Cambridge 1983.

Scobie, Edward, *Black Britannia: A History of Blacks in Britain*, Chicago Publishing Co., Chicago 1972.

Solomos, John, *Race and Racism in Contemporary Britain*, Macmillan, London 1989.

Verba, Sidney, Nie, Norman and Kim,J., *Participation and Political Equality*, Cambridge University Press, Cambridge 1978.

Verba, Sidney, and Nie, Norman, *Participation in America: Political Democracy and Social Equality*, Harper and Row, New York 1972.

Wainwright, Hilary, *Labour: A Tale of Two Parties*, Hogarth Press, London 1987.

Waller, Robert, *Moulding Political Opinions*, Harris Research Centre, London 1988.

Young, Alison, *The Reselection of MPs*, Heinemann Educational, London 1983.

Articles

'African Makes Westminster Debut', *African Times*, 19-25 June 1987.

'Atkin Sacking Leaves Labour in Chaos', *Asian Times*, 8-14 May 1987.

Austin, Rita, Corbett, Robin and FitzGerald, Marian, 'Minority Report from the Working Party on Positive Discrimination', Labour Party Document, London, 30 May 1986.

Bellos, Linda, 'The Way to Combat Labour's Racism', *The Independent*, 1 May 1987.

Benton, Sarah, 'A Watershed For Black Politics', *New Statesman*, 24 April 1987.

Bevins, A., 'It's A Funny Old World', *The Independent*, 23 November 1990.

'Black People and the Labour Party', A Consultative Labour Party Document, Autumn 1984.

'Black Representation in the Labour Party', *Race Today*, September/October 1984.

'Black Section Briefing on the Bill Morris Proposal', *Caribbean Times*, 29 January 1988.

Black Section Newsletter, *National Black Sections Campaign Publication*, Autumn 1987.

'Black, White and British', *Newsweek*, 17 December 1990.

Bochel, John and Denver, David, 'Candidate Selection in the

Labour Party', *British Journal of Political Science*, Vol.13, January 1983, pp.45-60.

Carvel, John, 'Hattersley Calls for End to Black Sections Martyrdom', *The Guardian*, 1 May 1987.

Comfort, Nicholas, 'Labour Drops Sharon Atkins', *The Daily Telegraph*, 30 April 1987.

Crewe, Ivor, 'The Black Brown and Green Votes', *New Society*, 12 April 1979.

Driscoll, M., 'A Black Among the Blimps', *The Sunday Times*, 9 December 1990.

'Four Black Tribunes', *Asian Times*, 25 June 1987.

'Four Sign with Kinnock', *African Times*, 24-30 April 1987.

FitzGerald, Marian, 'Are Blacks an Electoral Liability?', *New Society*, 8 December 1983.

FitzGerald, Marian, 'Ethnic Minorities and the 1983 General Election', Commissioned Report for Runnymede Trust, December 1983.

FitzGerald, Marian, 'Labour's Black Mark', *The Guardian*, 8 May 1987.

Greater London Council, 'Survey of Political Activity and Attitudes to Race Relations', Four Reports, 1985.

Gunn, S., 'Tories Try for Black Vote', *The Times*, 4 December 1990.

Hall, Stuart, 'The Gulf Between Labour and Blacks', *The Guardian*, 15 July 1985.

Harris Research Centre, *Political Attitudes Survey*, June 1987.

Harrison, Mark, 'A New Era: Will There Be a Black Caucus', *The Voice*, 16 June 1987.

Hill, D. and Mullin, J., 'Black, Blue and Bruised', *The Guardian*, 4 December 1990.

Howe, Darcus, 'Blacks in Parliament: No Great Expectations', *Race Today*, October/November 1984.

'ITN Exit Poll - General Election of 1987', Harris Research Centre, 11 June 1987.

King, Anthony, 'The Rise of the Career Politician in Britain', *British Journal of Political Science*, Vol.II, July 1978, pp.249-85.

Layton-Henry, Zig, 'The Importance of the Black Electorate', *Shakti*, June 1983.

Layton-Henry, Zig, 'The Tories: In Two Minds Over Race', *New Society*, 24 August 1978.

Layton-Henry, Zig, and Studlar, Donley T., 'The Electoral Participation of Black and Asian Britons: Integration or Alienation?', *Parliamentary Affairs*, Vol.38, Summer 1985, pp.307-18.

Le Lohé, Michael J., 'Voter Discrimination Against Asian and Black Candidates in the 1983 General Election', *New Community*, Vol.11, Autumn/Winter 1983, pp.101-8.

Linton, Martin, 'The Colour of Your Money Beats Racial Prejudice at the Polls', *The Guardian*, 19 June 1987.

Linton, Martin, 'Black, Hopeful, but "not Stereotypes" ', *The Guardian*, 2 June 1987.

'Listen to Sharon', *Caribbean Times*, 4 March 1988.

Masani, Zareer, 'The New Black Politics', *New Statesman*, 30 April 1982.

McAllister, Ian, and Studlar, Donley T., 'The Electoral Geography of Immigrant Groups in Britain', *Electoral Studies*, June 1984.

Modood, Tariq, 'Who's Defining Who?', *New Society*, 4 March 1988.

Morgan, R., 'Victory for Labour Blacks', *The Times*, 5 October 1990.

Morris, Bill, 'Time for New Thinking in the Black Sections Debate', *Caribbean Times*, 22 January 1988.

Mullin, J., 'Local Tories May Reject Black Candidate', *The Guardian*, 5 December 1990.

'Our Time Has Come', *Caribbean Times*, 19 June 1987.

Phillips, Mike, 'Wooing the Black Electorate', *New Statesman*, 20 April 1979.

'Political Attitudes Survey of Non-White Voters in Britain', Harris Research Centre, Conducted for the *Caribbean/African/Asian Times*, 25-29 May 1987.

Reiss, Charles, 'Thatcher Resigns!', *Evening Standard*, 22 November 1990.

Rule, S., 'Tories in Uproar Over Black Candidate', *New York Times*, 6 December 1990.

Sieghart, Mary Ann, 'A Deep Division but a Pointless Row', *New Statesman*, 24 April 1987.

Sweeney J., 'Black Tory Struggles to Crack the White Man's Code', *The Observer*, 9 December 1990.

Timmis, Nicholas, 'Black Candidates Get Their Chance at Last', *The Independent*, 5 June 1987.

Travis, A., 'Expulsion Call Over Tory 'Nigger' Jibe', *The Guardian*, 4 December 1990.

Upshal, David, 'From Tree-Shaking to Jelly-Making: Profile of Bill Morris', *New Socialist*, May/June 1988.

Upshal, David, 'The Labour Party: An Anti-Racist Dilemma', *New Socialist*, December 1987.

Upshal, David, 'Which Way Forward For Black Politics', *New Society*, 4 March 1988.

Webster, Philip, 'Labour Row as Kinnock Sacks Black Militant', *The Times*, 30 April 1987.

'Westminster's Changing Face', *The Voice*, 16 June 1987.

White, Michael, 'Major: We Unite to Win', *The Guardian*, 28 November 1990.

White, Michael, 'Thatcher: I Fight to Win', *The Guardian*, 22 November 1990.

Whiteley, P., 'Who are the Labour Activists?', *Political Quarterly*, Vol.52, April/June 1981, pp.160-70.

Wintour, Patrick and Knewstub, Nikki, 'Black Groups Win Own Organisation', *The Guardian*, 5 October 1990.

Young, Hugo, 'The Iron Lady Falls: Why Thatcher's Revolution Will go on Without Her', *Newsweek*, 3 December 1990.

Unpublished Documents

FitzGerald, Marian, 'The Emergence of Black Councillors and MPs in Britain', Conference Paper, University of Warwick, 26 November 1987.

FitzGerald, Marian, 'Black Sheep: Race in the 1987 Election Campaign', Unpublished Conference Paper, University of Essex, October 1987.

Lashley, Horace, 'An Analysis of the Successes and Failures of Black Candidates in the 1987 General Election', Conference Paper, University of Warwick, 26 November 1987.

Layton-Henry, Zig, 'The Black Electorate and the General Election of 1987', Unpublished Conference Paper, University of Warwick, 26 November 1987.

Layton-Henry, Zig, 'Black Electoral Participation: An Analysis of Recent Trends', Unpublished Conference Paper, Plymouth

Polytechnic, 12-14 April 1988.

Myers, Bernard, 'Black Britain and the Struggle for Parliamentary Political Power', Unpublished Thesis, Princeton University, 18 April 1986.

Rowley, Chris, 'The Campaign for Black Sections in the Labour Party', Unpublished Thesis, University of Warwick, April 1986.

Interviews

[All interviews were conducted by the author.]

Diane Abbott, MP Hackney North and Stoke Newington, at the House of Commons, 25 February 1988.

Ron Anderson, former Campaign Agent Brent South Labour Party, at the Brent South Labour Party Office, 2 June 1987.

Linda Bellos, former Labour Leader of Lambeth Council, at Lambeth Town Hall, 14 March 1988.

Paul Boateng, MP Brent South, at the House of Commons, June 1987, 28 May 1988 and 19 April 1990.

Ben Bousquet, 1987 Labour parliamentary candidate for Kensington, London, 26 February 1988.

Andrew Carnegie, former Labour Councillor in Lambeth, at Lambeth Town Hall, 25 February 1988.

Frank Crichlow, Mangrove Community Association, 13 June 1990.

Nirj Deva, 1987 Conservative parliamentary candidate for Hammersmith, London, 11 February 1988.

Roy Evans, former Member of the SDP National Executive Committee, London, 20 June 1990.

Zerbanoo Gifford, 1987 Liberal parliamentary candidate for Harrow East, 30 January 1988.

James Goodsman, Head of Community and Legal Affairs, Conservative Central Office, 14 June 1990.

Bernie Grant, MP Tottenham, at the House of Commons, 28 June 1988 and 29 March 1990.

Jonathan Hall, former Press Officer Brent South Labour Party, June 1987.

Richard Hume, former Secretary of Brent South Labour Party, June 1987.

Jebb Johnson, Director of the Mangrove Trust, 14 June 1990.

Dorman Long, former Labour Leader of Brent Council, 20 February 1988.

Joel O'Loughlin, National Black Caucus, 24 April 1990.

Lord David Pitt of Hampstead, at the House of Lords, 30 June 1988 and 22 June 1990.

Russell Profitt, 1987 Labour parliamentary candidate for Lewisham East and Educational Officer London Borough of Southwark, London, 11 February 1988.

Joyce Sampson, Conservative Party Member and London Liaison Chair for the One Nation Forum, 20 April 1990.

Phil Sealy, former Race Relations Advisor for London Borough of Lambeth, at Lambeth Town Hall, 10 March 1988.

John Taylor, Conservative parliamentary candidate for Cheltenham (1992) and for Birmingham Perry Barr (1987), 6 February 1988 and 19 April 1990.

Marc Wadsworth, former Chair of Black Sections, London, 12 March 1988.

Mike Wongsam, Chair of Black Sections, 16 August 1990.

Keith Vaz, MP Leicester East, Leicester, 22 December 1987.

Index

St Hill, Chris, 157

Taylor, John, 66, 69, 70, 72-3, 135, 139, 141, 143, 155, 156, 163, 164, 165
Tebbit, Norman, 57, 58
Thatcherism, 59-62, 122, 155
Thatcher, Margaret, 51, 58, 59-62, 64, 122, 124, 126, 160, 163
trade unions, 29, 39, 47, 89, 96, 104, 116, 123, 124, 132, 138

United Colored People's Alliance, 41
Upsal, David, 96

Vagrancy Act 1824, 52
Vaz, Keith, 13, 72, 112, 114, 135, 138, 141, 144, 145, 148, 158, 164
voluntary sector, 35, 53, 54

voting, 30-1, 32, 33, 83, 149

Waddington, David, 70
Wadsworth, Marc, 100, 116
Wainwright, Hilary, 82, 90
Wedderburn, Robert, 11
West Indian Standing Council (WISC), 39, 40, 47, 50
West Indies, 15, 37, 82
Williams, Shirley, 77
Wilson, Harold, 40, 90
Women's Sections, 26, 89, 101, 104, 118
Wongsam, Mike, 116

X, Malcolm, 45
X, Michael, 41

Young, Lord, 65
Youth Sections, 26, 89, 101, 104, 118